ENDLESS NIGHTS

ENDLESS NIGHTs

THE SANDMAN

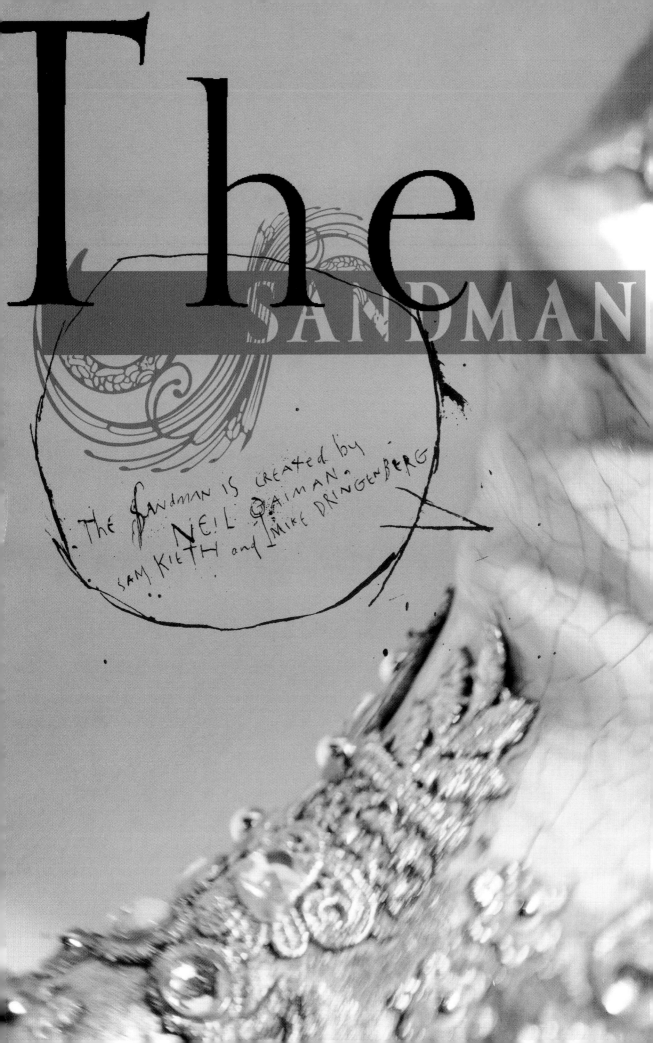

The SANDMAN

THE SANDMAN IS CREATED BY NEIL GAIMAN, SAM KIETH and MIKE DRINGENBERG

*For Jenette, for Paul, and especially for Karen
for trusting me.*
—Neil

THE SANDMAN: ENDLESS NIGHTS
Published by DC Comics, 1700 Broadway, New York, NY 10019.
Copyright © 2003 DC Comics. All Rights Reserved.
VERTIGO and all characters featured in this issue, the
distinctive likenesses thereof and related indicia are
trademarks of DC Comics. The stories, characters and
incidents mentioned in this magazine are entirely fictional.

Printed in Canada.
DC Comics, a Warner Bros. Entertainment Company.
First Printing.

Hardcover ISBN 1-4012-0089-3
Softcover ISBN 1-4012-0113-X

CONTENTS

All stories written by
Neil Gaiman.
All stories lettered by
Todd Klein.

Chapter 1 **DEATH** page 10
P. Craig Russell
artist
Lovern Kindzierski
colorist/separator

Chapter 2 **DESIRE** page 35
Milo Manara
artist

Chapter 3 **DREAM**
page 57 **Miguelanxo Prado**
artist

Chapter 4 **DESPAIR** page 79
Barron Storey
artist
Dave McKean
designer

Chapter 5 **DELIRIUM** page 100
Bill Sienkiewicz
artist

Chapter 6 **DESTRUCTION** page 122
Glenn Fabry
artist
Chris Chuckry
colorist/separator

Chapter 7 **DESTINY** page 142
Frank Quitely
painter

INTRODUCTION by Neil Gaiman

I.

Between 1987 and 1996 most of my working moments, and all of my sleeping ones, were given to telling one story, that of *The Sandman*.

Sandman came out more or less monthly, starting at the end of 1988. The story is collected in ten volumes, and two or three peripheral volumes, and an illustrated book which contained a retelling of an old Japanese folktale I completely made up. The story also spawned a Companion, and, more recently, an illustrated guide. Yesterday, in a hotel lobby in Turin I was asked if I could tell the story of the Sandman in twenty-five words or less. I pondered for a moment:

"The Lord of Dreams learns that one must change or die, and makes his decision," I said.

It's true, as far as it goes, although it leaves out quite a lot. Introductions always do.

II.

When I was done with *Sandman*, people asked if I would ever come back to those characters. Would I ever tell more stories about Morpheus, the King of Stories, or about his family, the Endless?

Sure, I said. One day.

This volume exists because there were artists I wanted to work with, and stories I wanted to tell, and because sometimes you look up and realize that one day is now.

III.

I've only worked with one of the artists in this book before: P. Craig Russell. Our *Sandman* story "Ramadan" was one of my favourites of the individual *Sandman* issues, and it gained a peculiar notoriety by being discussed and mentioned in newspapers around the world when Baghdad fell once more in 2003.

Craig's story is the first one I wrote for this book. I was alone in Venice, the week after September 11th 2001, the day the towers fell, and I found myself pondering the nature of time and of death.

Death is the second oldest of the Endless. It's hard not to love her. She loves you, after all.

Milo Manara has been an artist whose work in comics I've admired for many years: his graphic novel *Indian Summer*, written by Hugo Pratt, is one of the high points of the comics medium. The notion that Manara would draw me a tale of Desire was one of the things that carried me into the book you are now holding.

The story itself was loosely inspired by a historical anecdote mentioned by George MacDonald Fraser.

I met Miguelanxo Prado in 1996, in the Andalusian town of Gijon (graffitied by the locals, on road signs, to Xixon). In Gijon, or Xixon, the mists come off the Atlantic in the morning rendering the town entirely imaginary. When I saw Prado's art I knew I wanted to write something for him to draw.

Chronologically, this is the earliest Sandman story I've ever told. While it is true that I am someone who prefers mysteries to explanations, I found it pleasurable here to explain a number of things.

It would be several hundred million years before Death would cheer up, and longer than that before Delight became Delirium.

The Despair we meet in this story is the first Despair.

Barron Storey is a San Franciscan, an artist, a teacher, an illustrator, and a member of the Brotherhood of the Black Dog. His influence in the world of art has been enormous. I met him through Dave McKean, and soon found myself proposing that we create a big story of small stories together, to be called 25 Portraits of Despair.

I think, on reflection, that it is probably a good thing that we only created 15 Portraits of Despair.

Barron and I would both like to thank Dave McKean for his astonishing design and typographical work on the portraits.

Bill Sienkiewicz is someone I have known for at least sixteen years, and I've admired his work for longer than that. Many, many years ago we plotted a story together: a book of full-page images, which we would call *Obsessional*, in which the entire population of Manhattan, consumed by their own madnesses and desires and obsessions, joined a glorious carnival parade through New York and were eventually swallowed by the East River. The story would have been written by a man obsessed with the parade.

It's one of the best stories we've never told.

Delirium's story in this book is also fed by madnesses although Delirium inhabits the center of it, and not the periphery. The man in white is sometimes called Daniel, although he is more properly Dream. The dog is called Barnabas.

Delirium is the youngest of the Endless.

Glenn Fabry gained international renown for his cover paintings to Garth Ennis and Steve Dillon's *Preacher*, and I was delighted when he was able to make the time to draw the Destruction tale.

When R.A. Lafferty (who wrote like an angel, and, like most things angelic, may not be to everyone's taste) died in March 2002, he proved himself a poor predictive science fiction writer by several weeks, having already listed his year of death, in a 1983 essay, as being 2001. When I heard he had died I sat and read an old interview with him, in which he mentioned an idea that he had never managed to make into a story, and which he offered to the world. I thought it might be a fine memorial to a fine writer to see what I could do with that idea, and I named the peninsula San Raphael after Lafferty as well.

Destruction walked away from his family over four hundred years ago. Still, family ties are hard to break.

While the stories in this book can be read in any order (or none), Destruction's story follows Delirium's.

Finally, Frank Quitely concludes the Endless Nights with an eight-page tale about Destiny, which, it seemed to me when I had finished writing these stories, was a theme they had in common.

I've never met Frank Quitely. I always knew he was good. I didn't know he was this good.

IV.

I have spent the last month travelling across Europe on behalf of a book, being interviewed. In some countries they ask me how I feel about always being known primarily as the author of *Sandman*. (They only ask this in countries where I am known primarily as the creator of *Sandman*. There are countries where they ask me how I feel to be known primarily as a children's book author, or a fantasy writer. In Poland the first question always seemed to be how it felt to be known primarily as a post-modernist...)

And when they ask me that question, I tell them that Sandman is the biggest thing I've ever written, somewhere in excess of two thousand pages. That nothing I've ever written, or, I expect, ever shall write, matches it for scale.

I tell them it's nine years of my life. I tell them I'm proud. Not proud of myself, but proud of what I, and all the artists, and Todd Klein, and Danny Vozzo and the editors managed to bring into the world. People remember big things.

V.

If this is your first encounter with the world of the Sandman, it is worth bearing in mind that the Endless are not gods, for when people cease to believe in gods they cease to exist. But as long as there are people to live and dream and destroy, to desire, to despair, to delight or go mad, to live lives and affect each other, then the Endless will be there, performing their functions. They do not care a jot whether or not you believe in them.

The days are short, and are too soon over.

The nights, for good or bad, can seem endless.

Writing these stories was like coming home.

Neil Gaiman
Torino/Paris May 24, 2003

Chapter 1
DEATH

Death and Venice
art by P. Craig Russell

Here, where the darkness closes over me, like canal-water or the grave, I tell this story.

THEY USED UP THEIR FUTURE AS THEY USED UP THEIR PAST, TAKING EVERYTHING IN ONE LONG DAY, OVER AND OVER.

THE COUNT, TO WHOM THE PALAZZO BELONGED, HAD DECIDED THAT IT WAS HIS DESIRE TO BE CRUSHED TO DEATH BY A BULL ELEPHANT, BETWEEN TWO BEAUTIFUL VIRGINS, AT THE MOMENT OF ORGASM.

IT WAS AN IMMEDIATE JOKE MADE BY ALL ON THE ISLAND THAT THE VIRGINS WERE HARDER AND MORE EXPENSIVE TO PROCURE THAN THE ELEPHANT, ALTHOUGH, IN FACT, THE REVERSE WAS THE TRUTH.

THE ELEPHANT SWAM TO THE ISLAND AHEAD OF THE COUNT'S OWN SKIFF, AND LANDED AT EXACTLY 3:00 PM.

AT 3:02 PM A FLOCK OF SNOW-WHITE DOVES ROSE INTO THE AIR AND FLEW ACROSS THE ISLAND.

THE COUNT CONFERRED WITH HIS FRIENDS, HIS CONFIDANTES, HIS SERVANTS, HIS MISTRESS, AND EVEN, RELUCTANTLY, WITH HIS WIFE, TO ESTABLISH WHETHER HIS ELEPHANT-BORNE ECSTATIC DOOM WOULD BE BEST POSITIONED AT THE BEGINNING OR THE END OF THE NIGHT'S FESTIVITIES.

THE **END,** FOR WHAT COULD POSSIBLY FOLLOW IT?

THE **BEGINNING,** MY LORD, TO INSPIRE US ALL TO **REVEL** AND **REJOICE** AND **LOVE** AND **LIVE.**

12

I walk past echoing canals as green as old glass, houses shuttered and older than sin...

...and I hear bells— church bells, striking the hour...

...and the shrill blips and bleeps of mobile phones.

I have forgotten most of the Italian I learned in my childhood, which means that most of the voices I hear around me are companionable, reassuring, but not relevant. I do not try and make sense of what I hear.

Even when what I hear becomes a tinny, relentless techno version of the Macarena.

HEY. YOU AMERICAN? YES, *LADY?* YOU ARE WATCHING THE PUPPETS *DANCE?* HERE, LET ME SHOW YOU HOW THEY DANCE ON THE AIR.

YOU SEE THE MAGNETS ON *FEET?* AND MAGNET ON HEAD? THEY FEEL THE MUSIC, THEY *DANCE*. LIKE DANCING COKE CAN.

YES?

ONLY FIVE DOLLAR EACH.

OH! THESE ARE JUST SO *CUTE*. AND WHAT DO I *DO* TO MAKE THEM DANCE?

JUST PUT THEM CLOSE TO SPEAKERS, PLAY MUSIC, THEY WILL DANCE. *ONLY* FIVE DOLLAR.

FOR *YOU*, TEN FOR FORTY DOLLAR.

THEY ARE THE *CUTEST* THINGS. MY GRANDCHILDREN WILL *LOVE* THEM...

EXCUSE ME. SORRY TO BUTT IN, BUT IF YOU TAKE THEM HOME FOR YOUR KIDS, THEY WON'T DANCE. IT'S JUST AN ILLUSION.

HE IS *MAD*.

GO *AWAY* MAD MAN.

THERE'S A *MOTOR* IN THE DUFFEL BAG. A *MONOFILAMENT LINE* RUNNING FROM THE BAG TO THE BOOMBOX. THE PUPPETS HANG ON THE LINE AND ARE JERKING UP AND DOWN.

IS *MAGNETS!*

NO *MAGNETS*. NO *MAGIC*. JUST STRING SO FINE YOU CAN'T SEE IT WHEN IT'S MOVING. BUT IF YOU *WANT* TO PAY FIVE DOLLARS EACH FOR PAPER DOLLS, YOU GO AHEAD.

I SEE. THANK YOU, YOUNG MAN.

EH. *THIS* IS HOW I EARN MY *LIVING*. PLEASE. LEAVE ME *ALONE*.

He has a point. There are worse ways to earn a living. I leave him be.

NOTHING WAS EATEN FOR LUNCH THAT DAY BUT STALE BREAD, AND DRIED FISH, AND WATERED WINE.

A DEPUTATION FROM THE PALAZZO VISITED THE MONASTERY ON THE NORTHERN SHORE OF THE ISLAND...

...AND A TROUPE OF MONKS, HUMORLESS AND HOLY MEN, EVERY ONE OF THEM, FILED UP TO THE PALAZZO AT 2:00 PM.

AT 3:02 PM A FLOCK OF SNOW-WHITE DOVES ROSE INTO THE AIR AND FLEW ACROSS THE ISLAND.

THE CONFESSIONS WERE HEARTFELT, AND ACCOMPANIED BY TEARS.

AND ONCE CONFESSED, THE PENITENTS KNELT, TO BE SCOURGED UPON THEIR NAKED BACKS, FLOGGED UNTIL THEIR SKIN WAS LACERATED AND BLOOD RAN ACROSS THE PALAZZO'S MOSAIC FLOOR.

AND NO MAN THERE, AND NO WOMAN WAS MORE PENITENT...

...MORE HONEST, SHED SO MANY TEARS...

...OR SO MUCH BLOOD,...

...AS THE COUNT HIMSELF.

THEY PRAYED...

...AND THEY WAILED,...

...AND THEY REPENTED,...

...AND THEY BLED UNTIL MIDNIGHT.

A MARVELOUS END TO A PERFECT DAY.

They've been parting visitors from their money for so long here in Venice that they can't help but be good at it. Normally, they give value for money. That last encounter left a sour taste in my mouth. They didn't cheat the tourists when I came here as a boy.

And that starts me remembering once again.

I have remembered this too much; so now I can no longer be sure whether it is the event that I am remembering, or my memory of the event.

A hot, still day. Lizards, on the side of a brick wall, watch me warily.

I had been staying with my aunt and uncle, with my cousins. My Italian was not good, but I could make myself understood, and we all spoke some English.

You could catch them, if you were fast enough. But if you grabbed them by the tail it would break off, wriggling in your hand, while the lizard ran away.

We loaded the picnic food and the bottles of fruit-juice and the wine into my Uncle's vaporetto, the water-taxi he drove, and we travelled out into the lagoon until we reached the island.

There are many islands in the Venice Lagoon. Over the years they have all been inhabited, my Uncle told me as I proudly steered the boat. But times change. He pointed out the islands that hold factories, barracks, munitions, convents, as we passed.

I remember the slosh, slosh, slosh of the water against the side of the motorboat.

WHEN I WAS A YOUNG MAN, IN THE ARMY, WE WERE STATIONED ON THIS ISLAND. ON THE NORTH SIDE IS AN OLD MONASTERY.

NOW IS ALL RUINS. BUT IS A GOOD PLACE FOR A PICNIC.

YOU KEEP AWAY FROM THE RUINS. THEY WILL BE DANGEROUS.

YES, UNCLE.

We all ate bread and fish and fruit and chocolate. We drank apricot juice, the adults drank wine. Then my Aunt and Uncle sat beneath an old fig tree and read a book or dozed, and sent us to play, with one final warning to keep well away from any ruins.

We played hide-and-seek across the southern half of the island, clambering over ruined walls.

I grew bored with the game, or perhaps my cousins had hidden themselves too well.

I kept walking...

HELLO, SERGEI.

HAVE YOU SEEN ANY OTHER **KIDS** AROUND HERE, LIKE ME? WE WERE **PLAYING**.

I HAVEN'T SEEN ANY-BODY HERE IN A **LONG** TIME.

It didn't seem strange to me that she knew my name, or that she talked my language.

WHAT ARE YOU DOING?

WATCHING THAT GATE. I'M WAITING FOR THE DAY THAT IT OPENS.

WELL, WHY DON'T YOU JUST GO **AROUND** IT?

THAT WOULDN'T BE **FAIR**. AND WHAT MAKES YOU THINK THAT I'D REACH THE SAME **PLACE** IF I WENT AROUND IT?

IT'S LOCKED.

OR IT'S RUSTED SHUT.

IT WON'T OPEN.

20

I CAN WAIT.

MMM FFF

SERGEI!

WHERE **WERE** YOU?

WHY DIDN'T YOU **COME** WHEN WE **CALLED?**

WE LOOKED FOR **HOURS!** PAPA IS **FURIOUS!**

Somehow, it was nearly dark. I had been missing for hours. I said I had fallen asleep, and perhaps it was true. I was in disgrace, and remained so for the remainder of my stay.

In time, I came to believe I had imagined the whole thing. And now, on two weeks' leave from my unit, I am in Venice once again.

21

AT NINE IN THE MORNING, THE COUNT AROSE AND DECLARED FOR THAT EVENING A MASKED BALL OF UNPARALLELED SPLENDOR AND MAGNIFICENCE.

CASKS OF SHERRY WERE BROUGHT UP FROM THE CELLARS, ALONG WITH BOTTLES OF THE FINEST WINES.

ANIMALS WERE SLAUGHTERED AND SPITTED.

COSTUMES WERE EXAMINED, MASKS WERE PURCHASED AND REPAIRED. THE WORD WAS SENT TO VENICE, AND THE SURROUNDING ISLANDS.

AT 3:02 PM A FLOCK OF SNOW-WHITE DOVES ROSE INTO THE AIR AND FLEW ACROSS THE ISLAND.

AT DUSK, A FLOTILLA OF BOATS, EACH WITH A LANTERN IN THE PROW, PULLED UP IN THE BAY...

...DISCHARGING SEVERAL DOZEN WOMEN, MASKED AND EXQUISITELY DRESSED.

NOBLEWOMEN! SOME WHISPERED.

COURTESANS! SAID OTHERS.

NUNS, FROM THE CONVENT OF SAN MICHELE DI MURANO, HERE IN DEFIANCE OF THEIR VOWS...

WHISPERED THOSE WHO HAD SCULLED THE OARS.

DOES THIS VAPORETTO GO OUT TO THE ISLANDS?

IT GOES *ANYWHERE*, AS LONG AS YOU *PAY.* YOU WANT A TOUR OF THE ISLANDS?

MY BROTHER CAN MAKE YOU GOOD DEAL FOR GLASS ON *MURANO.*

I told him which island I wanted him to take me to, then described where it was to the best of my recollection.

MM. IF YOU WISH. BUT IT IS DESERTED. THERE ARE NO STORES, NO RESTAURANTS, *NOTHING* FOR A VISITOR TO SEE. AND IN THIS WEATHER...

I KNOW.

I'LL PAY.

So he took my money, and the vaporetto, the water taxi, sped through the canals of Venice on its way to the lagoon.

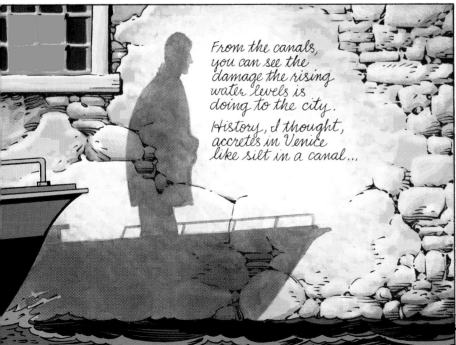

From the canals, you can see the damage the rising water levels is doing to the city.

History, I thought, accretes in Venice like silt in a canal...

...and it laps against the bricks and rocks and the deep wooden piles.

And as we ride, I find myself wondering: If my life would have been different—if, say, I had not gone to the island as a boy.

Would I have stayed with Patricia?

Would I have joined the army, applied for the unit I applied for?

Perhaps I would still be with Patricia, if, at each kiss, at every touch, I had not compared her to the woman on the island.

Her eyes were not so dark and sparkling.

Her smile was never so haunting.

I channel that longing for something I cannot reach into my job. I do it efficiently.

Someone has to.

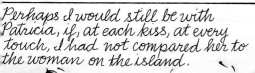

I tell the vaporetto driver to wait for me.

HELLO. YOU CAME BACK, I THOUGHT YOU WOULD.

Everything moved slowly when I saw her. The rain seemed to fall gently, like snowflakes.

YOU KNOW, I ALMOST THOUGHT I HAD IMAGINED YOU.

NO. I'M REAL.

DO YOU COME OUT HERE EVERY DAY? OR DO YOU LIVE HERE ON THE ISLAND?

I GET AROUND. YOU KNOW, YOU'RE THE FIRST PERSON EVER TO COME BACK.

DO YOU REMEMBER WHAT YOU DID THE LAST TIME YOU WERE HERE?

I TRIED TO OPEN THE GATE.

WOULD YOU LIKE TO TRY AGAIN?

YOU KNOW, THERE'S PROBABLY SOME LAW PROTECTING HISTORICAL REMAINS.

I pulled. It was set fast into the brick. I was angry with myself, I thought, I should have brought a sledge-hammer, or a crowbar, or a wrecking ball.

Then I thought to kick it.

I was kicking at my life.

At my family.

At my unit.

At death, at time, at every lie I had ever been told.

At every paper doll jiggling on its invisible string ...

YOU **DID** IT!

WHERE ARE WE?

MAY THE 23rd, 1751.

THAT'S A **WHEN**, NOT A **WHERE**.

HERE, IT'S A **WHERE**.

CAN YOU WAIT HERE?

I HAVE BUSINESS INSIDE.

I WANT TO COME **WITH** YOU.

OKAY, I GUESS.

YOU WANT TO BLEND IN, DON'T YOU? COME ON, LET'S SPOIL THE PARTY.

YOU LOOK MOST *LOVELY*, YOUNG LADY.

WILL YOU WALK WITH ME?

ONLY FOR A *LITTLE* WHILE, GIUSEPPE, YOU DIED OF SYPHILIS IN 1768, IN AN ATTIC IN TRIESTE.

HE DROWNED IN A STORM.

SHE DIED IN CHILD-BIRTH.

AS AN OLD MAN, HE CHOKED ON A BONE IN A BOWL OF FISH SOUP.

YOU PLAY CHESS **WELL**, MARIE, BUT YOU DO NOT PLAY AS WELL AS **I** DO.

WE SHALL SEE, MY LORD. **ONE** OF US SHALL PAY THE PRICE TONIGHT.

MY **LORD!** THERE ARE PEOPLE **DYING!**

THEN TIDY THE BODIES AWAY, OR MAKE AN ARTISTIC ARRANGEMENT OF THEM, DO NOT DISTURB ME.

NO, MY LORD, THEY **DECAY.** THEY CRUMBLE TO DUST...

AH. THAT WILL BE ALL, MY **DEARS.**

BUT YOU **PROMISED!** YOU PROMISED THAT WE WERE **FREE** FROM **TIME** HERE!

PLEASE, ENOUGH.

MY **LORD!** WE HAVE CAPTURED **INTRUDERS.** A STRANGER, AND HIS WOMAN. BOTH OF THEM ARE DRESSED IN **BLACK.**

SO...

YOU ARE **TIME. FOUL TIME,** WHO **STEALS** THE GOLD FROM A MAIDEN'S HAIR AND **TAKES** THE SAPPHIRE FROM A CHILD'S EYES.

DARK TIME, WHO HAS STOLEN FROM **EVERY** THING THERE EVER WAS THE THINGS THAT IT HELD PRECIOUS AND DIVINE...

...AND LEFT **NOTHING** BUT MEMORIES AND ASHES AND THE GRAVE.

I SEALED THAT GATE **MYSELF.** I BARRED TIME FROM THIS PLACE, AND FORCED YOU TO OBEY MY EVERY WHIM.

WHAT'S HE **SAYING?** I DON'T **UNDERSTAND.**

IT'S JUST A SPEECH HE WROTE FOR TONIGHT. THE USUAL STUFF. YOU AREN'T MISSING ANYTHING.

...MY WISDOM AND MY MAGIC AND MY POWER. AND IF WE DIED TODAY, **SO WHAT?**

TOMORROW WOULD BE **ANOTHER** PERFECT DAY. AND NOW, ALTHOUGH MY DAY IS ENDING, **STILL** I SHALL GAIN MY IMMORTALITY AS THE MAN WHO SLEW **TIME HIMSELF,** AND FREED US ALL FROM HIS PROFOUND EMBRACE--!

NOW HE'S SAYING THAT HE'S GOING TO KILL YOU.

BUT THIS ISN'T **HAPPENING,** IS IT? I MEAN, WE'RE SEEING THE **PAST.**

NO, THIS IS **NOW.** IT'S JUST ANOTHER **KIND** OF **NOW.**

ENOUGH.

TOMORROW, YOU VANISH.

SOME SAY THE COUNCIL OF TEN TAKES YOU...

...SOME SAY THE INQUISITION.

YOU ARE NOT TRIED.

YOU SIMPLY VANISH.

SEVERAL MONTHS FROM NOW A CORPSE WITH NO FACE, NO HANDS, NO FEET, WILL BE PULLED FROM THE GRAND CANAL.

"THIS PLACE WILL GET A VERY BAD REPUTATION. IT WILL REMAIN UN-INHABITED, AND THEN, IN THE 1820s, IT BURNS TO THE GROUND."

30

SIGNOR? YOU ARE SLEEPING?

ARE YOU *UNWELL?* SHALL I TAKE YOU BACK NOW?

I cannot speak. I nod.

He takes my arm, and leads me across the rubble, as if he is leading a very old man.

A flock of white doves flies above us, through the mist, like the souls of the dead...

...and then they, too, leave the island.

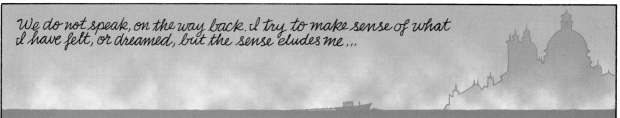

We do not speak, on the way back. I try to make sense of what I have felt, or dreamed, but the sense eludes me...

When I get back to the city everything seems thin and unreal. I stare at the tourists, and I wonder what goes on behind the eyes, inside their heads, inside their worlds.

I know that in my heart.

One last time.

I shall see her again.

Until then, I shall continue to send people to her.

Next week, I return to my unit.

The people in the city seem paper thin in the mist.

They believe they are dancing to the music of their lives...

But, I think, like the puppets, each of us is pulled upon invisible strings, until the night comes, and we are put away.

I shiver, and hurry from the square, as the darkness of the city closes over me, like canal water or the grave.

Chapter 2
DESIRE

What I've tasted of Desire

art. by **Milo Manara**

I SAW THAT BOY YOU LIKE. HE WAS KISSING A GIRL. I COULD *SEE* THEM.

I *DON'T* LIKE HIM. I DON'T KNOW WHY YOU KEEP SAYING THAT.

SISTERS KNOW. SISTERS KNOW *EVERY-THING.*

I COULDN'T TELL YOU WHEN I FELL IN *LOVE* WITH HIM. TO TELL THE TRUTH, I DON'T THINK I COULD EVEN SAY FOR CERTAIN WHEN I FIRST BECAME *AWARE* OF HIM.

WHICH IS *FUNNY,* ISN'T IT? CONSIDERING EVERYTHING THAT HAPPENED AFTERWARDS.

IT *CERTAINLY* WASN'T LOVE AT FIRST SIGHT. NOR WAS IT THE *HATE* THAT BLOSSOMS INTO LOVE.

WHEN I HEAR SOME YOUNG WOMAN GOING ON ABOUT HOW MUCH SHE HATES A YOUNG MAN, I THINK, *THERE'S WEDDING GARLANDS IN THEIR FUTURE.*

"BUT THE *BEST* I WAS EVER ABLE TO MANAGE FOR *HIM* WAS A MILD DIS-LIKE. IT WAS HIS *SMILE*--TOO COCKSURE BY HALF--OR HIS LOPING WALK LIKE A WOLF WITH MILES TO TRAVEL."

AND MOST IRRITATING OF ALL WAS THE WAY THE OTHER GIRLS THOUGHT HE WAS--"

SWEET!

GORGEOUS!

TASTY!

FUNNY!

--THAT LEFT ME FEELING NOTHING FOR HIM AT ALL.

"SOME OF THEM DESIRED HIM FOR HIS SKILL IN BATTLE--FOR IN THOSE DAYS THERE WERE ALWAYS BORDER SKIRMISHES, AND WOLVES ATTACKING IN THE WINTER--AND HE TOOK HEADS AND PELTS AS EASILY AS HE TOOK HEARTS."

WE'D MEET, OF COURSE, AND TALK, IN THE WAY YOU DO, AS IT WAS NOT A BIG VILLAGE--A FEAST HALL, AND HOUSES THAT SURROUNDED IT, INSIDE A WALL. YOU COULDN'T HELP MEETING PEOPLE.

"THERE WAS *ONE* MORNING WE WALKED TOGETHER, HIM ON HIS WAY DOWN TO THE BROOK TO FISH, ME TO SEE TO THE GOATS, AND THE MIST WAS THICK, SO WE WALKED *CLOSE,* AND WE TALKED-- NOT ABOUT MUCH.

"HE TOLD ME HIS FATHER, OUR CHIEF, SAID THAT THE GODS DID NOT COUNT TIME SPENT *FISHING* IN THE HOURS OF A MAN'S LIFE...AND I SAID THAT WAS VERY *INTERESTING,* ALTHOUGH I THOUGHT IT WAS *UNLIKELY,* ALL THINGS CONSIDERED."

AND WHEN WE CAME TO SAY *GOOD MORNING* AND *FARE-THEE-WELL,* I COULD THINK OF *NOTHING* I WANTED MORE THAN TO SPEND THE REST OF MY *LIFE* WITH THAT *INFURIATING* YOUNG MAN...

...WITH HIS *COCKSURE* SMILE AND HIS *WOLFISH* WALK.

"HE NEVER SEEMED TO NO-TICE ME, THOUGH, AFTER THAT DAY.

"AND THEN IT WAS *SPRING*, AND IT SEEMED LIKE EVERY TIME I TURNED AROUND I'D FIND HIM PRESSED UP AGAINST A TREE WITH ANOTHER OF THE VILLAGE GIRLS."

"AND I CRIED AT NIGHT, OF COURSE, EVEN IF ALL I HAD TO *COM-FORT* MYSELF WITH WAS THE KNOWLEDGE THAT THE GIRLS SEEMED TO MEAN NO *MORE* TO HIM THAN THE FISH IN THE BROOK."

BUT *KARA*, SHE'S A *WITCH*. YOU CAN'T WANT HIM *THAT* MUCH!

I WANT HIM SO MUCH *MORE* THAN THAT.

"THERE'S TIMES WHEN YOU'VE GOT TO TAKE YOUR HEART IN YOUR HAND, SO I WALKED OUT ONTO THE MOOR, AND I TOOK HER GOAT-CHEESE AND SAUSAGES, AND IN HER LITTLE ROOM I TOLD HER I NEEDED HIM."

SO YOU'RE AFTER A *LOVE POTION?*

I'D NOT **WANT** A MAN I COULD **BUY** WITH A POTION. AND I **DON'T** BELIEVE THAT ANY OF YOUR POTIONS WORK.

HEE. WELL, THEY DON'T **NOT** WORK. THEY BUY A GIRL OR A BOY THE CONFIDENCE TO MAKE A FIRST MOVE-- TO **LOOK** OR TO **TOUCH** OR TO **SMILE**, WHERE OTHERWISE THEY'D JUST LOOK AWAY AND **SIGH**.

SO IF IT'S NOT A POTION YOU WANT, WHAT **IS** IT?

I WANT HIM TO WANT **ME** AS MUCH AS I WANT HIM.

THERE ARE **GODS** AND **GODDESSES** YOU COULD PRAY TO, OR SACRIFICE TO. THEY'LL DO **ANYTHING** FOR A LITTLE **BLOOD** SPILLED ON THE RIGHT **STONE**.

I'VE NEVER CARED FOR GODS OR GODDESSES. THEIR GIFTS DON'T COME FREE.

NOTHING COMES FREE, GIRL. STILL...THERE IS ONE **OTHER** YOU COULD TALK TO.

MAN, OR **WOMAN?**

BOTH, PERHAPS. OR **NEITHER**. LOOK FOR GOLDEN EYES. WAIT UNTIL YOU FEEL YOUR **HEART** BEING TUGGED WITH A **LONGING** THAT HAS NOTHING TO DO WITH YOUR YOUNG MAN.

FOLLOW YOUR **HEART**.

HE WENT SOUTH, TO THE TOWN ON THE COAST WHERE THE SHIPS CAME IN TO BUY TIN FROM THE MINES. THERE WAS BUSINESS TO BE DONE THERE.

"HIS FATHER, OUR CHIEF, LED SEVERAL OF THE VILLAGE ELDERS TO NEGOTIATE WITH THE FOLK FROM ACROSS THE RIVER. WE DID NOT CARE FOR THEM."

MY OWN MOTHER HAD BEEN BORN ACROSS THE RIVER, AND WAS STOLEN IN A RAID WHEN SHE WAS FIFTEEN, AND *SHE* ALWAYS SAID IT WAS THE *BEST* THING THAT EVER HAPPENED TO HER.

"THE *NEGOTIATIONS*, FOR GRAZING RIGHTS, FOR AMBER, FOR THE RANSOM OF PRISONERS, WENT *BADLY.*

"SO BADLY THAT HIS FATHER AND THE WHOLE NEGOTIATING COMMITTEE WERE SENT BACK ACROSS THE RIVER IN *PIECES.*

"AND WHEN I HEARD THE NEWS, I BOUND MY BREASTS AND PUT UP MY HAIR AND JERKIN, AND I SET OFF FOR THE COAST."

"I WAS HALF A DAY'S TRAVEL FROM THE VILLAGE, AND HAD SEEN NOBODY ON MY TRAVELS WHEN I REALIZED THAT THERE WAS A MAN COMING TOWARDS ME.

"WELL, I THOUGHT IT WAS A MAN, THEN I WASN'T SO SURE, FOR THERE WAS SOMETHING DAINTY ABOUT HIS FINGERS, SOMETHING CAT-LIKE IN HIS WALK.

"AND WHEN I CAME CLOSE I COULD SEE THAT HIS EYES, LIKE A CAT'S, WERE GOLDEN.

"'AND I HEAR YOU'VE BEEN LOOKING FOR ME,' HE SAYS.

"'I SUPPOSE,' I SAID. 'I SUPPOSE I MIGHT HAVE BEEN.'

"'WELL THEN,' HE SAYS, 'COME INTO MY PARLOR...'

"AND WITHOUT A BEAT, BETWEEN ONE MOMENT AND THE NEXT, WE WERE...I DON'T KNOW WHERE WE WERE."

AM I DREAMING?

NOT A BIT OF IT. QUITE THE REVERSE, IF ANYTHING.

WE TALKED FOR WHAT SEEMED LIKE AN AGE. SO MUCH OF WHAT HE SAID I DID NOT UNDERSTAND;

SO MUCH MORE OF IT I HAVE FORGOTTEN.

HE TALKS ABOUT *STORIES*. MY *BROTHER*. LET ME TELL YOU THE *PLOT* OF *EVERY* ONE OF HIS DAMNED STORIES. *SOMEBODY WANTED SOMETHING. THAT'S* THE STORY. MOSTLY THEY *GET* IT, TOO.

MOST PEOPLE WANT THINGS LIKE A *CANDLE-FLAME,* FLICKERING, SHIFTING. *YOU,* ON THE OTHER HAND, *WANT* LIKE A *FOREST FIRE.*

I SHOULD *WARN* YOU, GETTING WHAT YOU WANT AND BEING *HAPPY* ARE TWO QUITE DIFFERENT THINGS.

I *KNOW* THAT.

WILL YOU *GIVE* ME WHAT I WANT?

SO WHAT *WILL* YOU GIVE ME?

OF COURSE NOT.

A *SMILE,* AND I'LL SAVE YOU A FEW DAYS TRAVEL.

YOU'RE MARKED AS *MINE.* BUT THEN, YOU ALWAYS *WERE.*

AND WHAT DO *YOU* WANT FROM *ME?*

EVERYTHING. WHAT *ELSE* IS THERE TO WANT?

44

"AND THEN, WITHOUT A BREAK, I COULD SMELL THE SEA-SCENT, AND HEAR THE CAW OF GULLS. AND I WAS WALKING DOWN A NARROW LANE AT DUSK.

"I WALKED INTO THE FIRST HALL I SAW--HOSPITALITY TO STRANGERS WAS PART OF OUR CREED--AND I SAID:

YOUR FATHER'S **DEAD.** IT'S TIME TO COME HOME.

WHO **KILLED** HIM?

THEM OVER THE RIVER.

WHERE ARE YOU **GOING?**

BACK TO THE **HILLS.** TO RULE MY **PEOPLE.**

WHAT ABOUT **ME?**

YOU'LL FIND **SAILORS** WITH GOLD ENOUGH IN THEIR WALLETS, AND **MERCHANTS** WITH SHIELDS AND SHOES AND PAINTED SHELLS, AND YOU'LL NOT WEEP FOR ME.

COME ON, **LAD.** LET'S GO HOME.

WE WALKED. THE FIRST DAY, HE SAID NOT A WORD.

"THAT NIGHT THE RAIN CAME. WE ATE BY THE FIRE. I WATCHED HIM LOOKING AT THE RAIN AND THE SKY, AND HIS FACE WAS WET."

YOU ARE THE *GOAT-GIRL*... I DID NOT *KNOW* YOU. *WHY* DID I NOT KNOW YOU?

YOU WERE *DISTRACTED*.

WHY DID *YOU* COME TO TELL ME MY FATHER WAS DEAD? WHY WASN'T A *MAN* SENT?

I'M SURE THEY SENT A MAN. BUT I CARED THE MOST. I GOT TO YOU *FIRST*.

"HE LOOKED AT ME WITH NEW EYES, THEN."

YOU ARE A WOMAN. I AM A MAN. LET US DO THE THING THAT MAN AND WOMAN DO.

LET'S *NOT*.

I DO IT *WELL*. YOU WILL HAVE NOTHING TO COMPLAIN ABOUT.

SO THEY SAY.

DON'T YOU *WANT* ME?

I WANT YOU MORE THAN THE SUN WANTS THE MOON. MORE THAN A FISH NEEDS THE RIVER. MORE THAN A HEART NEEDS TO BEAT. YOU ARE ALL THAT I DESIRE.

THEN--

THEN I SHALL CONTINUE TO SAY *NO*. AND *YOU* WILL PLACE YOUR SWORD BETWEEN US TONIGHT, TO SHOW THAT YOU WILL LAY NO FINGER UPON ME UNLESS I *ASK* YOU TO. AND I SHALL NOT ASK.

SO THAT'S HOW IT *IS*, EH?

THAT'S HOW IT IS.

46

SO. I'VE ASKED YOU TO MAKE LOVE TO ME. YOU SAID *NO.* NOW I ASK YOU TO *MARRY* ME.

AND GRATEFUL IT IS I AM THAT YOU HAVE ASKED, AND *JUST* AS GRATEFULLY DO I DECLINE.

WHY, IN THE NAME OF ALL THE GODS?

BECAUSE IF YOU MARRY ME SIMPLY TO *QUENCH* YOUR DESIRE, THEN WHEN YOU HAVE HAD YOUR FILL OF ME, YOU'LL BE *DONE.*

A *KISS,* THEN?

NOT EVEN *THAT.*

YOU'VE *CHANGED.* WHO HAVE YOU BEEN TALKING TO?

"AND I SAID *NOBODY,* ALTHOUGH I KNEW WHO I HAD BEEN TALKING TO, AND HIS EYES--OR HER EYES-- WERE THE COLOR OF *GOLD.*"

"WHEN WE RETURNED TO THE VILLAGE THE FUNERAL REVELS BEGAN: THREE DAYS OF DRUNKENNESS AND SAGAS."

"I WENT UP TO THE HIGH FIELD, WITH THE GOATS, AND I WAITED."

HE WAS CHIEF OF THE CLAN, AND HE COURTED ME FOR THREE MOONS. HE BROUGHT ME *GIFTS*--NEVER ANYTHING USEFUL, MEN NEVER THINK LIKE THAT, BUT I SAID THANK YOU TO EACH GIFT.

"AND THEN ONE DAY HE RE-TURNED WITH HIS CHEEK ALL CUT, AND HE LAID A LINEN WRAP AT MY FEET."

IT BELONGED TO THE MAN WHO *KILLED* MY *FATHER.* I'LL PUT IT AROUND YOUR THROAT AT OUR WEDDING, IF YOU'LL *LET* ME.

THAT WOULD BE NICE.

"HUNCHBACKS DANCED AT OUR WEDDING, FOR LUCK. IT'S NOT SOMETHING YOU SEE ANY MORE.

"OUR WEDDING NIGHT...OUTSIDE THE HALL THEY CHANTED AND CRASHED PANS AND MADE SUCH A DIN.

"AND IN OUR ROOM, WE MADE LOVE LIKE *FLAMES*--OPENING, BLENDING, BURNING.

"WE MADE LOVE LIKE ANIMALS, LIKE GODS, LIKE DREAMS.

"WAS IT WORTH WAITING FOR? GODS, YES. IT WAS WORTH *WORLDS*, THAT NIGHT, WORTH *SOULS*, WORTH *ETERNITY.*"

"I KNEW WHAT THE VILLAGE GIRLS WERE SAYING--THAT HE'D BE BORED SOON, AND BACK IN THEIR BEDS.

"THEN THEY LAUGHED THAT HE'D BE THEIRS ONCE MY BELLY BEGAN TO SWELL."

IT'S A *PRETTY* FLOWER. I'LL WEAR IT BEHIND MY EAR UNTIL YOU COME BACK FROM THE COAST, AND I'LL *THINK* OF YOU.

I'LL BE *BACK* BEFORE YOU KNOW IT.

"IT HAD BEEN A HARD WINTER. THE WOLVES HAD BECOME BOLD, AND IF WE DID NOT GUARD OUR FLOCKS WE WOULD FIND THEM DEAD."

MY *LADY!* THERE ARE *MEN* AT THE GATES!

"MY HUSBAND HAD GONE TO A MEETING OF CHIEFS. THE MEN OF THE VILLAGE WERE OUT ON WOLF-WATCH, AND NOT DUE BACK UNTIL DAWN."

WE ASK FOR *HOSPITALITY.* WE HAVE TRAVELLED A LONG WAY THIS DAY, AND WE ARE *HUNGRY* AND *THIRSTY.*

OUR *HOSPITAL- ITY* IS YOURS.

I LET THEM IN. WHAT ELSE COULD I HAVE *DONE?* HOS- PITALITY TO STRANGERS AND TO FRIENDS. THAT WAS THE WAY OF IT.

PLEASE, BE SEATED. I SHALL SEND FOR *FOOD* FOR YOU. IT SHALL NOT BE SAID THAT WE DO NOT TAKE CARE OF TRAVELLERS. MY ONLY REGRET IS THAT MY *HUSBAND* CANNOT BE HERE WITH US TODAY.

THERE ARE *TEN* OF THEM. WE SHALL NEED A BARREL OF ALE. TWO LARGE *SALMON,* AND A HAUNCH OF COLD *VENISON*--AND SPIT A *LAMB* AND GET IT TURNING FOR *LATER.*

YES'M.

I'LL CARVE.

AH, *YOU* MUST BE THE LEADER. VERY WELL. *YOU* MUST CARVE FOR US ALL.

I AM AFRAID THAT OUR *BARD* IS OFF ON *WOLF-PATROL* WITH THE REST OF THE MEN, BUT I CAN SING TO YOU, IF YOU WISH? THEY SAY MY VOICE IS PLEASANT ENOUGH.

SHE SINGS *WELL.*

AYE. DID YOU SEE HOW SHE WAS *LOOKING* AT ME JUST THEN?

AT *YOU?* HAVE YOU NO *EYES* IN YOUR HEAD? IT WAS *ME* SHE SMILED AT...

YOU'RE *BOTH* MAD! IT'S *OBVIOUS* WHO SHE WANTS.

HAS SHE *SEEN?* YOU SAID IT WAS HER *HUSBAND'S* HEAD!

IT *IS!* SEE-- THAT'S MY *BROTHER'S* BAND SHE WEARS ABOUT HER NECK...I DON'T UNDER-*STAND...*

NOW, YOU MUST TELL ME, WHICH OF YOU IS THE MOST CUNNING IN BATTLE?

I AM!

NO, I AM!

WELL, LET ME SEE YOU WRESTLE. AND FOR THE WINNER...I'LL HAVE TO THINK OF SOMETHING NICE.

"I WATCHED THEM WRESTLE AND CURSE, I LISTENED TO THEM BRAG, AND I SMILED AT EACH OF THEM, ADMIRED EACH OF THEM--BUT NEVER TOO MUCH.

"THEIR LUST WOULD HAVE BEEN HARD TO CONTROL. BUT THEIR DESIRE...AT THAT MOMENT, I COULD PLAY DESIRE LIKE A HARP. EACH OF THEM WANTED ME. EACH OF THEM WANTED ME TO WANT HIM...

"TIME PASSED SO QUICKLY.

"THEY JOKED, THEY SANG, THEY RECITED LONG SAGAS. THEY FOUGHT, NAKED, WITH KNIVES. THEY DRANK, THEY STUFFED THEIR FACES WITH MEAT AND WIPED THEIR FINGERS ON THEIR HAIR AND BEARDS."

AND THEN IT WAS DAWN, AND OUR MEN CAME BACK AND SLAUGHTERED THEM LIKE WOLVES.

WERE YOU NOT *AFRAID?*

NO.

BUT THEY HAD KILLED YOUR *HUSBAND.*

YES.

I AM HIS WIFE, AND THE LADY OF THIS VILLAGE. IT WOULD BE A *POOR* THING IF I COULD NOT BEND A MAN TO MY DESIRE.

BURY HIM.

AND THAT WAS WHEN I KNEW I'D NEVER SEE HIS *COCKSURE* SMILE AGAIN, OR HIS *LOPING* WALK. AND I KNEW THAT THERE WAS NOTHING LEFT THAT I WANTED.

I'D *HAD* ALL I WANTED. AND IT WAS *GONE.*

AND I KNEW THERE WAS NOTHING ELSE I *COULD* WANT AS I HAD WANTED HIM. TIME WENT BY, AND THE YEARS, AND THE MONTHS, AND THE DAYS.

I MARRIED AGAIN. A MAN ASKED ME. I COULD THINK OF NO REASON NOT TO. WE HAD CHILDREN. *FINE* CHILDREN.

I WAS ALIVE, THAT ONE NIGHT, HOLDING THOSE MEN IN MY HAND. IF YOU HAVE *NOTHING* LEFT TO *WANT,* THEN YOU JUST *WAIT* UNTIL THERE'S NOTHING LEFT TO *WAIT* FOR, DON'T YOU?

I WATCHED THE CHILDREN GROW TALL, AND LOVE AND WANT, AND I WONDERED IF *THEY* HAD LOVED AS *I* HAD LOVED. IF *ANYONE* EVER HAD.

A *LONG* TIME AGO I MET SOMEBODY WITH *GOLDEN EYES.* I WAS TOLD SO *MANY* THINGS. BUT THEY ARE GONE NOW.

AND SOMEBODY SAID... THAT IT BURNED...

LIKE A FOREST FIRE...

MANARA

56

Chapter 3
DREAM
The Heart of a Star
Miguel Jones

The Heart of a Star art by **Miguelanxo Prado**

WILL YOU TELL ME A STORY, FATHER? BEFORE I GO BACK TO SLEEP?

OF COURSE. LET ME SEE... THIS ALL HAPPENS LONG AGO.

HOW LONG AGO?

IMAGINE TIME. IMAGINE ALL THE TIME THAT THERE EVER WAS, ALL THE TIME THERE EVER WILL BE. IN THIS TOTALITY OF TIME, A HUNDRED THOUSAND YEARS IS AN EYEBLINK, A MILLION YEARS PASSES LIKE A SIGH.

AND EVEN IN THAT TOTALITY OF TIME, THIS TAKES PLACE A LONG TIME AGO...AND FAR, FAR AWAY.

WHEN KILLALLA OF THE GLOW GETS AGITATED, GREEN FLAMES BEGIN TO FLICKER ABOUT HER BODY.

SHE IS AGITATED NOW, AND THE FLAMES ARE LEAPING AND COLDLY-BURNING LIKE BRUSHFIRE.

THIS IS *SILLY*.

SHE CONCENTRATES; WITH HER WILL, SHE FORCES THE GREEN FLAME INTO A POINT WHICH DANCES AND BURNS ON HER FINGER-TIP, READY TO DO HER BIDDING.

Hello, Killalla.

AAAAH!

OH. IT'S *YOU*, DARLING. YOU SCARED ME.

I apologize.

But who else could it have been, in this place, Killalla?

I--I DID NOT *KNOW*. I DO NOT NORMALLY TRAVEL ACROSS THE VASTNESS OF SPACE IN A BUBBLE, TO MEET MY LOVER'S FAMILY AND HIS FRIENDS.

I am very pleased to hear it.

WHAT WILL THEY THINK OF ME?

They will treat you with respect, I trust.

TELL ME MORE ABOUT THE *WORLD* WE ARE GOING TO.

It is not a world. It is a palace...

...and we are almost there.

You can see it for yourself.

As Killalla described it, long after, in a book that was, for a few hundred thousand years, and across a dozen worlds, considered sacred, it was as if, for a heartbeat, she was surrounded by something huger, hotter, brighter than the mind could bear.

And then it was a palace, huge, yes, and vaster than she had dreamed a single place could be, and beautiful as any jewel, its towers burning like diamonds in the darkness of space.

DREAM! YOU ARE MOST WELCOME HERE, AT MY LITTLE PARLIAMENT. YOU HONOR US ALL WITH YOUR ATTENDANCE.

AND WHO IS **THIS**, WHO BRIGHTENS MY HUMBLE HOME WITH HER LOVELY PRESENCE?

This is Lady Killalla of the Glow, Mizar.

AN HONOR, LADY.

Are my family here yet?

NOT **ALL** OF THEM. **DESTRUCTION** IS HERE, BUT HE IS IN HIS QUARTERS, AND SO IS **DELIGHT. DESIRE** HAS BEEN HERE SINCE LAST NIGHT.

DESTINY SENDS APOLOGIES, BUT HE WILL NOT BE COMING.

Destiny does not often leave his garden.

But Desire is already here! My love, you must meet Desire. My favorite sibling, if such a thing is possible. So funny and so kind.

DESIRE IS IN THE PLAZA OF MIMIC-FLOWERS. I SHALL ACCOMPANY YOU THERE.

LADY, PLEASE, FEEL FREE TO EAT OR DRINK OR TOUCH WHAT**EV**ER YOU WISH. ANYTHING HERE IS SAFE FOR YOU.

ALL THAT IS HERE IS FOR YOUR ENJOYMENT.

THANK YOU.

Desire.

HELLO, DREAM.

I owe you thanks, my sibling, inadequate thanks, and so much more. How can I ever repay what you have given me?

WELL, PERHAPS YOU SHOULD BEGIN BY *INTRODUCING* US.

Of course. This is Lady Killalla of the Glow. From one of the young worlds--hers is called Oa. She is one of the five high (priest-artist-police-entities) of her culture.

Killalla, this is my sister-brother, Desire.

SUCH A *PRETTY* THING. BLUE SKIN. WHAT A PLEASANT CONCEIT.

THERE. LOOK AT *ME*, EVERYONE. I HAVE BLUE SKIN *TOO!*

LORD DREAM...? A MOMENT OF YOUR TIME?

Certainly, Rao. If you two will excuse me, for a moment...?

OF COURSE, BROTHER. GO AND DO YOUR SILLY BUSINESS.

TELL ME, SWEET GIRL, *HOW* DID YOU MEET MY BROTHER?

AH. FOR GENERATIONS, MY PEOPLE HAVE BEEN STUDYING THE INTERSECTION OF FORCE AND WILL, AND HOW WE COULD *HARNESS* IT, AS LIGHT, TO IMPROVE THE UNIVERSE.

WATCH....

WE HOPE THAT *ONE DAY* WE WILL BE ABLE TO HARNESS THE POWER OF THE GLOW *PERFECTLY...*

...AT THIS MOMENT, THE FIVE OF US CONTROL THE GLOW, EXPLORING IT WITH OUR WILL AND OUR HEARTS, USING IT TO SHOW US THE UNIVERSE...

SOME DAYS AGO, I WONDERED WHAT WOULD HAPPEN IF I COMMANDED THE GLOW TO ACCOMPANY ME INTO MY *DREAMS--*

--AND THEN, IN MY DREAM, YOUR BROTHER APPEARED.

OF *COURSE* HE DID.

WHY WOULD HE THANK YOU FOR... FOR THE WAY WE MET?

BECAUSE HE *WANTED* YOU. WELL, HE WANTED *SOMEONE.* HE WAS LONELY. BECAUSE YOU WANTED HIM.

BECAUSE HE BELIEVES THAT I DID HIM A *FAVOR.*

WHAT LOVELY *ROOMS!* SO BEAUTIFUL! HOW *OLD* IS THIS PLACE, MY SWEET?

A day. Two at most.

Mizar made it for the conference. Once the conference is done, it will dissolve into pure light and cosmic dust.

SHE *MADE* THIS?

WHEN I THINK OF THE ENERGY AND THE CONCENTRATION IT TAKES TO MAKE ONE SMALL THOUGHTFORM... AND TO MAINTAIN IT...

Mizar has power to spare.

They are about to start...

SHOULD *I* ATTEND THIS PARLIAMENT?

I would not advise it. It is a deathly dull business, chiefly concerning zones of responsibility and the merits of obligation. But you should attend the gathering at the fountains.

WHAT A MAG**NIF**ICENT PLACE!

RAO! EVERYONE, THIS IS **RAO**--MY FAVORITE RED GIANT!

HOW **DID** YOU GET THE ENDLESS TO YOUR PARLIAMENT, MIZAR?

PERSISTENCE, MOSTLY. I DECIDED SEVERAL HUNDRED THOUSAND PULSES BACK THAT WE NEEDED TO CONFER, TO SET BOUNDS. AND AFTER THAT IT WAS SIMPLY A MATTER OF FOLLOWING UP. TRYING TO KEEP IT EXCLUSIVE, YET BRING THE **PERFECT** MIX OF BEINGS TOGETHER...

I--I'M **SORRY.** REALLY AWFULLY...OH DEAR. I DIDN'T MEAN TO.

HE'S ONE OF YOUR PERFECT MIX?

HE'S VERY, **VERY** YOUNG. HE'S CALLED **SOL.** HE MAKES ME **LAUGH.** AND HE **MEANS** WELL.

I WAS INVITED. I HAVE COME. MAKE OF THAT WHAT YOU WILL.

WE ARE HONORED, LADY.

I AM MAKING YOU UN-COMFORTABLE.

NO, LADY. NOT AT ALL.

I SHALL LEAVE. DECIDE WHAT YOU LIKE AT YOUR PARLIAMENT. IT IS ALL ONE TO ME. IT WON'T MAKE A LOT OF DIFFERENCE, IN THE LONG RUN, WILL IT?

ONE BY ONE, YOU WILL ALL COME TO ME.

It begins. Feel free to walk the gardens. You can return to our rooms merely by wishing it.

YOU MEAN *ALL* I HAVE TO DO IS--

OH.

WHAT ARE *YOU*?

I AM CALLED KILLALLA OF THE GLOW.

YOU ARE VERY PRETTY. AND YOU HAVE A NICE NAME. BUT WHAT *ARE* YOU?

HOW DO YOU *MEAN*, WHAT *AM* I?

WELL, I *MEAN*... WHAT I *MEAN* IS, WHAT ARE YOU?

LIKE, UM, ARE YOU A SUPERINTELLIGENT COSMIC CLOUD FORMATION, OR A DIMENSION THAT HAS INCARNATED LIKE THAT OR A STAR OR WHAT?

I'M...I'M A *FEMALE*. THAT MEANS I BEAR THE YOUNG OF MY SPECIES. I COME FROM A PLANET CALLED *OA*. I AM...

YOU MEAN YOU REALLY *ARE* JUST WHAT YOU *LOOK* LIKE YOU ARE.

YES.

WELL, *THAT'S* PRETTY WEIRD. WHY ARE YOU HERE THEN? DO YOU *OWN* THE MILKY WAY OR SOMETHING?

NO. I'M HERE WITH DREAM OF THE ENDLESS. I'M HIS COMPANION.

OH.

OOPS.

I...

OOOOHHHH. I'M SORRY. I SHOULD HAVE *REALIZED*. I AM SO *EMBARRASSED*. I THINK I'M JUST GOING TO HIDE UNDER THE TABLE UNTIL I'M NOT EMBARRASSED ANY MORE.

DON'T BE SILLY--

PLEASE, COME OUT OF THERE.

IN A MINUTE.

ARE YOU HIS GIRL-FRIEND?

I....I DON'T KNOW. MAYBE.

I THOUGHT YOU WERE HERE ON BUSINESS.

NO. HE JUST WANTED ME TO MEET HIS FAMILY. I MET DESIRE ALREADY.

AND YOU MET ME, TOO. I'M DELIGHT.

HOW DO YOU DO?

I....I'M NOT CERTAIN. I THINK I DO OKAY. HAVE THEY STARTED TALKING? THE PEOPLE AT THE THINGIE?

I BELIEVE SO.

I SHOULD GO THERE. YOU KNOW WHAT THEY WILL BE SAYING? BLAH BLAH BLAH BLAH. THAT'S WHAT THEY ARE GOING TO SAY.

BLAH BLAH BLAH BLAH BLAH.

OKAY, I WENT.

LA LALA LA...

GREETINGS, LADY.

HELLO MIZAR.

I THOUGHT YOU PEOPLE WERE HAVING YOUR MEETING.

THE MEETING HAS BEEN MOMENTARILY SUSPENDED, ON A POINT OF ORDER.

I DON'T CARE IF YOU *ARE* A DIMENSION OR *NOT*. IF YOU'RE TOO SMALL TO BE *PERCEIVED*, THEN I *DON'T* THINK YOU GET TO ADDRESS THE ASSEMBLY.

IT'S NOT A *SIZE* THING. IT'S A MATTER OF PERCEP-TION AND RESPECT.

YOU SHOULD COME AND LISTEN. YOU MIGHT FIND IT INTERESTING.

YOU HAVE MET YOUR...DREAM'S BROTHER, DESTRUCTION? HIS IS THE PROCESS THAT FUELS ALL THE STARS. WITHOUT HIM, ALL WOULD BE LIFELESS AND DARK.

NO. WE HAVE NOT MET. I AM KILLALLA OF THE GLOW.

A LOVELY THING *INDEED!* I HOPE MY BROTHER KNOWS WHAT HE HAS IN YOU. WE HAD *ALL* HOPED THAT HE MIGHT FIND SOME-ONE TO SHARE HIS EXISTENCE WITH. INDEED, DESIRE UNDERTOOK--

NO. I SPEAK OUT OF TURN.

THE HEARTS OF STARS MAY BE MY *DOMAIN,* BUT EVEN THE HEARTS OF STARS... NO, AGAIN, I MISSPEAK. I AM NOT ONE FOR FINE WORDS, OR PRECISE WORDS. LET ME CLARIFY, LITTLE ONE.

GREAT ONES? A COM-PROMISE HAS BEEN REACHED. IT BEGINS ONCE MORE...

THANK YOU, SOL.

WILL YOU ANSWER ME A QUESTION, KILLALA OF THE GLOW?

SHOULD I...*KNOW* YOU?

NOT EXACTLY. I AM DREAM'S OLDER BROTHER. SOME CALL ME DESTINY.

OH.

CAN I GET YOU SOMETHING TO EAT?

I SHALL NOT BE HERE FOR LONG.

YOU ARE BLIND.

YES.

WOULD YOU LIKE ME TO MAKE YOU EYES, WITH THE GLOW?

THIS PLACE IS SO BEAUTIFUL, IT IS SUCH A SHAME, YOU NEVER SEEING IT.

I THANK YOU, BUT NO.

KILLALLA, DO YOU *LOVE* MY BROTHER?

I DO NOT *KNOW*. I *THINK* SO.

YOU ARE A MORTAL WOMAN.

MILLENNIA FROM NOW, IT WILL BE DECIDED THAT THE ENDLESS MAY NOT LOVE MORTALS. YOU WILL BE DISCUSSED AND REMEMBERED AND TALKED ABOUT MANY TIMES IN THOSE DISCUSSIONS.

HE LOVES ME?

HE LOVES ME?

THE WAY *I* SEE IT NOW, FAERIE WON'T BE A *DIMENSION* SO MUCH AS AN *ASPIRATION.* DO YOU SEE?

MM. WILL IT BE TIED TO ANY PARTICULAR SUN-SYSTEM?

NOT AS *SUCH.* IT WILL NEED A CERTAIN QUALITY OF LIGHT ONE SIMPLY CANNOT GET FROM YOUR PEOPLE...

YOU KNOW, I DON'T REALLY HAVE ANY PLANETS. WELL, I *DO,* BUT THEY'RE ALL ASLEEP. NOTHING THAT HOLDS LIFE.

BUT I WAS THINKING THAT MAYBE WHEN THEY WAKE AND MAKE LIFE, I THOUGHT, A DOMINANT LIFE-FORM COULD LOOK LIKE *YOU.*

YOU HAVE SUCH... GRACE.

THANK YOU, SOL...ER, I THINK.

KILLALLA! KILLALLA OF THE *GLOW!* SOL, YOU DON'T MIND IF I INTRUDE?

I'VE BEEN WANTING TO TALK TO YOU FOR THE *WHOLE* OF THE CONFERENCE.

ER...

YOU *KNOW* ME?

OF *COURSE* I DO! DON'T YOU KNOW ME? YOU ARE ONE OF MY FAVORITE PEOPLE.

YOU DO SEEM FAMILIAR...

...LIKE SOMEONE I'VE KNOWN ALL MY LIFE.

WELL, I SHOULD *HOPE* SO.

YOU KNOW, I'VE BEEN WALKING AROUND HERE FOR...FOR HOWEVER LONG IT'S BEEN, SMILING AND NODDING, AND I HAVE NO IDEA WHAT *ANYBODY'S* TALKING ABOUT.

THEY KEEP TALKING ABOUT *STARS* AND *DIMENSIONS* AND *GALAXIES,* AND MY...MY LOVER'S FAMILY--

YOU MEAN YOU REALLY DON'T *KNOW?*

DOES EACH OF YOU REPRESENT THE PEOPLE FROM A DIFFERENT STAR SYSTEM, OR SOMETHING...IS IT A PARTY, OR A BUSINESS MEETING OR A CON-FERENCE OR *WHAT?*

WELL, YES, IT'S ALL OF THOSE THINGS. BUT...

LOOK, YOU SEEM NICE ENOUGH. WILL YOU ANSWER SOME **QUESTIONS** FOR ME? JUST GIVE ME SOME STRAIGHT ANSWERS?

CERTAINLY.

WHY WAS EVERYONE **AFRAID** OF HIS OLDER SISTER? THE **PRETTY** ONE? THEY WOULDN'T TALK TO HER OR ANYTHING.

BECAUSE IN THE END, EACH SUN, EACH WORLD, EVERY GALAXY, WILL COLLAPSE AND END, EITHER INTO FLAME, OR INTO DARKNESS. AND WHEN THAT HAPPENS, SHE WILL BE THERE, FOR EACH OF US. **NOW** DO YOU UNDERSTAND?

NOT REALLY.

SHE IS DEATH.

OH.

YOU MEAN...SHE'S THE **GODDESS** OF DEATH, OR THE INCARNATION, OR...

NO. SHE **IS** DEATH. JUST AS THAT ONE IS DESIRE. OR YOUR LOVER IS DREAM.

OF COURSE HE IS DREAM. I MET HIM IN THE KINGDOM OF DREAMS, AND HE FOLLOWED ME BACK. HE'S THE **KING** THERE...

NO, KILLALLA. HE IS **NOT** THE KING. HE **IS** DREAM. JUST AS **I** AM STO-OA.

THAT'S A **SILLY** NAME. THAT'S WHAT CHILDREN CALL THE SUN ON THE WORLD WHERE I COME FROM. "THE LIGHT OF OA."

JUST BECAUSE A NAME IS USED BY THE YOUNG DOESN'T MAKE IT FOOLISH. I **AM** THE LIGHT OF OA, AFTER ALL, AM I NOT? I SHINE ON ALL OA, KILLALLA. SINCE YOU WERE A BABE, I GAVE MY LIGHT TO **YOU.**

N-NO.

NO! YOU ARE **NOT!**

KILLALLA...?

WE ARE THE *STARS.* WE DO NOT *REPRESENT* THEM. WE *ARE* THEM.

IT'S NOT...

BUT *HOW*--

NO. DON'T TELL ME. IT'S TOO BIG, EVEN TO *THINK* OF--I MEAN, YOU'RE A *STAR?* A SUN? *MY* SUN?

YOUR SUN, IF YOU'LL *HAVE* ME, KILLALLA.

I DON'T UNDERSTAND...

I THINK... I THINK HE **SAW** US.

WHY SHOULD THAT SCARE **YOU?** YOU ARE A **SUN.**

I AM A SUN, CERTAINLY. BUT HE IS **DREAM.** THEY SAY DEATH IS KINDER THAN HE IS.

WHAT SHOULD WE **DO?**

I DON'T KNOW.

DON'T LEAVE ME.

I NEVER SHALL.

THINK ABOUT IT, RAO. WOULDN'T BRINGING LIFE ONTO A PLANET THAT IS INHERENTLY UNSTABLE ADD TO THE BEAUTY OF THE LIFE? IF AT ANY MOMENT IT COULD EXPLODE...

I HAD NOT THOUGHT OF IT LIKE THAT.

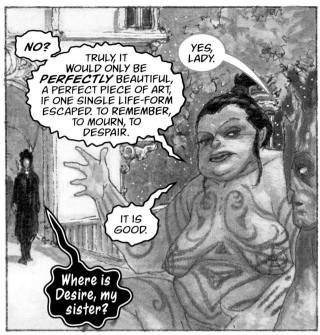

NO?

TRULY, IT WOULD ONLY BE *PERFECTLY* BEAUTIFUL, A PERFECT PIECE OF ART, IF ONE SINGLE LIFE-FORM ESCAPED. TO REMEMBER, TO MOURN, TO DESPAIR.

YES, LADY.

IT IS GOOD.

Where is Desire, my sister?

THERE. BY THE POOL.

Thank you.

Killalla of the Glow is with Sto-Oa.

YES. They were kissing.

THEY *WERE*. THEY'VE GONE FAR *BEYOND* THAT NOW. HIS HOT FINGERS ARE ALREADY INVADING HER SOFT CURVES AND MOIST CREVICES--

Enough! You find this funny?

ACTUALLY, YES.

I see. Then we are not friends, you and I, Sibling. Not any longer. Do not interfere further in my affairs.

IT WAS A *JOKE*.

DOESN'T HE HAVE A SENSE OF HUMOR?

NOT THAT I'VE EVER NOTICED.

Mizar?

YES, SIRE.

I have outstayed my welcome, and I shall be leaving now.

THE WOMAN YOU BROUGHT WITH YOU...?

Will find her own way home. I imagine that Sto-Oa will transport her; they are going to the same place, after all.

You. Sol. Did I hear you say you planned to have some of your planets inhabited?

WELL, I'D CERTAINLY *LIKE* IT. OBVIOUSLY, IT'S UP TO THE PLANETS THEMSELVES. NONE OF THEM HAVE WOKEN YET.

Yes. Their dreams are very lonely, and beautiful.

YOU *KNOW* THAT? OH. OF *COURSE* YOU DO. YOU KNOW, SIRE, YOU ARE ALWAYS WELCOME IN MY SYSTEM.

I know, Sol. One day...

AND WITH THAT, HE WAS GONE.

77

HE KNEW YOUR NAME, FATHER?

YES, CHILD.

WHEN I HAVE LIFE ACTUALLY WALKING AND DANCING AND DREAMING ON MY SURFACE, WILL THE ENDLESS COME TO ME, PROPERLY? WILL *DREAM* BE THERE?

YES.

POOR DREAM. AND WHAT HAPPENED TO HER? TO KILLALLA OF THE GLOW?

SHE DIED, AS THEY ALL DIE. THEY DO NOT LIVE LONG. BUT SHE MADE STO-OA HAPPY, FOR A MOMENT, AND ON HER DEATH HE TRANSLATED HER INTO HIS CENTER, TO BURN INSIDE THE HEART OF THE STAR AND COMFORT HIM THROUGH THE LONG NIGHT.

THAT'S GOOD. POOR STO-OA. POOR KILLALLA.

GO BACK TO SLEEP, MY DAUGHTER. REST AWHILE...

SLEEP UNTIL LIFE WAKES YOU.

Chapter 4
DESPAIR
Fifteen Portraits of Despair

DESPAIR

Fifteen
Portraits
of Despair
art by
Barron Storey
designed by
Dave McKean

15 Portraits of Despair

For Barron Storey

1

The first portrait.

Her eyes are grey.

Her hair is straggly and wet.

Her fingers are stubby.

The nails are chewed and broken.

Her teeth are crooked, jagged things.

There is a vacancy in her gaze, a feeling of absence when you are near her that is impossible to put into words.

Her sigil is the hooked ring.

One day her hook will catch your heart.

Describing her, we articulate what she is and why she is:

when hope is past, she is there.

She is in a thousand thousand waiting rooms and empty streets, in grey concrete buildings and anonymous hotels.

She is on the other side of every mirror.

When the eyes that look back at you know you too well,

and no longer care for what they see, they are her eyes.

She stands and waits, and in her posture the pain no longer tells you to live, and in her presence joy is unimaginable.

Mother's Boy Series, Number 3.

2

So when the Bishop's secretary said he wanted to see me, I knew it had to be something to do with the drinking. It's not that I'm a problem drinker. I'm Irish: son of a hundred generations of serious drinkers. But these days, the church needs to avoid even the apparency of wrongdoing.

I know a few priests go to A.A. I couldn't go as a cleric. It'd have to be "Hello Dermot," not "Hello Father Byrne," when I stood up to say my little bit.

And I've been letting things slide a little recently.

It wasn't the drinking. He said, ten years ago there was a girl. He showed me her picture. I said I remembered her: Odd little thing, always making up stories, wanting the attention.

She says you

   interfered

      with her,

          he says.

I told him I never.

   I could prove, it too,

      even after
      all this time.

No, he says. You cannot. We're paying her three quarters of a million, Dermot. And you need to reconsider your vocation. It's the insurance company, you understand.

But I never, I said again. And, and I'm a priest.

We need to be seen to be taking action, says the Bishops' secretary. We can't seem to be condoning this sort of thing. If you stay in the church, we'll have to report you to the police.

For what, I say?

Molesting young girls, he says sadly.

But I never, I told him, and I could hear the whine in my voice, like a dog you've kicked when you've had the one too many, who just can't get it into his head why.

This isn't fair, I said.

No, he says. But it's right.

And when I get to the door, thinking about trying not to cry, at my age, about starting all over at 54, about the bottle of Canadian Club in the bottom drawer of the desk in my study, I say, Father, think for a moment. What would Jesus do?

The Bishop's secretary shook his head. If he had to deal with the insurance companies, he'd probably hang you out to dry, same as the rest of us, he said, and he didn't smile.

She decides to make a list of the things that make her happy.
She writes 'plum-blossom' at the top of a piece of paper.

3

Then she stares at the paper,

unable to think of anything else.

Eventually it begins to get dark.

Eventually it begins to get dark.

4

It starts with a cat twining against your leg, two, maybe three years ago, just after you hurt your leg, and it's a stray, and you put down milk in a saucer for it, and when you live in a damn trailer on the edge of the town you can be glad of the company and hell the kittens were cute and you put down more milk and pretty soon don't it seem like all the money you're collecting on disability is going to buy these sacks of catfood and you can hardly keep clear who is whose mother or brother or sister anymore and the trailer stinks of spray but you don't hardly notice it, because those cats are family and so it's a bitch when your brother-in-law over in Moose Hill says he's got you a job on the dairy farm there and it's three hundred dollars a week, and a place to stay, and that's the best money when you're nothing but a farmhand with a leg that's shot and you don't know what to do with the goddamn cats, the kittens in the drawers, sixty maybe even seventy cats and there's more now out in the fields who'll come back tonight to be fed.

Be here Friday, says your brother-in-law, or they'll get someone else in.
And that disability won't last forever.

So you lock the trailer door and you go, thinking maybe you'll be back at the weekend to feed
the cats, and knowing that you won't.

And then there's just the face on the sheriff's man as he tells you that they had to wear air masks
to go into the trailer, that five of them cats were somehow still alive, that sixty of them, maybe
more were found part eaten, and he waits for you to say something, anything, and you shake your
head and you don't say nothing at all.

❺ He collects his lover.

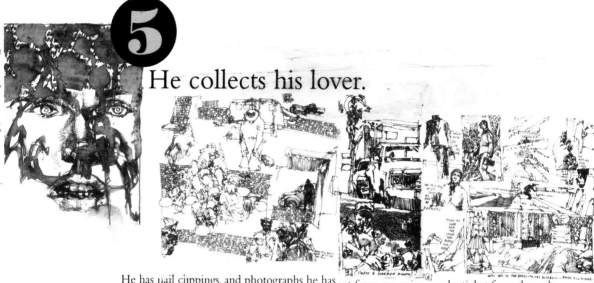

He has nail clippings, and photographs he has cut from magazines, and a ticket from the only tram journey they took together, to a late-night Chinese restaurant, where his lover was not recognized.

After sex, while his lover sleeps, he takes things, slips them into his bag, a tee shirt that smells like his lover, underpants, a dusty aspirin taken from his toilet kit.

His lover exists for him chiefly as a body in a sequence of hotel rooms.

In his bedroom he has made a small shrine to his lover: his greatest treasure is a knotted condom, retrieved from a waste bin, with the cold remains of his lover's seed congealed inside it.

Sometimes he does not see his lover in the flesh for months at a time. At night he watches his lover on the television.

"If you smile before the commercial break," he whispers to his lover, "it means you are thinking about me. If you blink now it means you love me, you truly love me, and one day you will come out here for always."

He buries his face in a tee shirt that no longer smells like anybody at all, and waits for his lover to blink.

❻

It wasn't the loving each other or the knowing they could never be together.

It wasn't the wind in the eaves of the empty house,
or the bone-dry rattle of the pills in the brown-glass bottle.

It wasn't the bitter taste, with only a stale box of red wine to wash it away.

It wasn't waking, with her dead and you all too alive.

It was the way your fingers shook. It was a stammer, and the thickness of your tongue
as you tried to speak. It was the sound of the sirens, coming closer.
It was knowing that you would never get another chance.

"Despair" with dolls

Despair remembers.

It is a peculiar, flat memery,
in which things become bleak and bounded by the dark.

1. 2. 3.

ENDLESS
DESPAIR

There is joy in there,
of course,
and love,
and touching.
The presence that makes the
present absence unbearable.

1. Truth.(Yellow) Our world is built on the injustices of the past.
2. Blood.(Red) All who live are brothers and sisters. All will die.
3. Earth.(Green) Mother of all.

Without triumph,
without love,
without joy,
her work would be for nothing.

To begin with, he lost his job.
It was not his fault.
It was an honest mistake.
You must believe me.

It was shame, then, not despair that moved him.
Each day he got up and showered and dressed,
he kissed his wife and babies, and drove away.

He spent the day in libraries,
or in the parked car, or walking.

He applied for jobs,
and was turned down.

When his severance pay ran out he slowly,
methodically, emptied his savings accounts.
He told his wife he had been promoted.

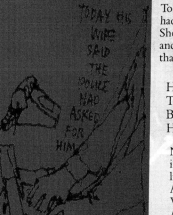

The first break-in was easy.
A wallet, jewelery.
No one was home.
No one was hurt.
It was practically a victimless crime.

Today his wife said that the police
had been by asking after him.
She told them that he was at work,
and they said that was odd,
that they thought he'd been let go.

He told her that people make mistakes.
That new girl on the switchboard.
But he wasn't feeling well.
He thought he'd stay home today.

Now he's in his bedroom,
in the empty house,
listening to someone pressing the doorbell.
And the bell.
Which rings.
And rings.
And rings.

9

Her kiss is the deep ocean.

Her kiss is not the deep ocean.
Her kiss is the grey sky.

Her kiss is a blind alley.

Her kiss is her touch is her breath
is her fingers is what remains
after the laughing is over.

HER KISS IS THE BLACKNESS. HER KISS IS NOT THE BLACKNESS.

WITH THIS PAIN
I THEE FEEL

Her kiss is the black dog that follows you in the darkness.

There is a black dog beneath the grey sky, by the blind alley, beside the deep ocean. It is not her kiss. Come closer....

10

And people ask,
does Despair despair,
does Dream dream,
does Desire desire?

It is simpler than that.
He is dream.
It is desire.
She is despair.
Take away the despair and there is nothing left.

Nothing but an empty room,
and a hook of the perfect shape
and size for snagging your heart.

It is a writer, with nothing left that he knows how to say.

It is an artist, and fingers that will never catch the vision.

12 He was not a rich man, and it took all he could raise from his fields, his house, his friends, to take the man to court. He has mortgaged his future for fairness, for relief, for Justice. What happened to his child was not right.

And now the judge comes out and his mouth opens and he explains the verdict, his words a tangle of legalities.

"What does he say?" the man asks his lawyer,

but already he knows, by the smiles in the eyes of his opponent. It is the same smile he sees on the faces of the lawyers on the other side. On the face of the judge.

He feels his lawyer's hand on his arm and he would have it be over. Have everything be over. But he knows it has only just begun.

siTTing in a gRave,
Reading a newspapeR.

Bank TelleR.

DRiving a cab.

MOON HOOK
HOOK THE MOON
MOON HOOKER
BARB HOOK
SUFFER. LINE AND
SUFFERAGETTE
TOY
DOLL SINKER
WINDOWS. FISHERS
PLANETS BE
IN MY MEN
BEDROOM
THERE ARE
UNIVERSES
OF
SUFFERING

visiTing a jail.

Fishing in a chuRch.

Playing fluTe in a sToRm.

A) If you can't be happy where you are, you can't be happy anywhere. Discuss, with examples from your own life.

B) Hell is Other People. Do you agree? Demonstrate how this might or might not apply in the case of:

i) The Armenian Massacres of 1915

ii) Either the life of Algernon Charles Swinburne or the death of Walt Disney

iii) the darkness before creation

(Answer two of three.)

C) Construct an analogy using the saline nature of either tears or the sea and the salt that makes a dish palatable and adds piquance and savour.

(Examinees are encouraged to refer to either the third daughter of Llyr or Lot's wife, but not both.)

D) If I was God I would abolish...............

Complete in 250 words or less. Physical practicalities and human nature are to be respected. The Law of Conservation of Happiness may not be violated.

(Counts for 50% of your final score.)

She had waited until her husband and children were far away, and had driven into the snowy woods, and ended it. Just let it all go.

She had wanted the pain to stop. The heart-hurt. She slept her way into death, only waking when the Highway Patrol found her body.

She was cold, rigid, frozen, when they found her.

Someone like that, said the patrolwoman. You'd think she'd have everything to live for.

She tried to speak, to tell them that that was what made the pain unbearable but, like someone caught in a bad dream, she could not make herself heard. She screamed, and no sound came out. She watched as they took her body away.

She sat by the side of the road, in the snow, all bodiless and afraid, waiting for the happiness to start.

To be Despair. It is a portrait.

Only close your eyes and feel.

Chapter 5
DELIRIUM
Going Inside ...with Bill Sienkiewicz

Chapter 5

DELIRIUM

Going Inside

art by **Bill Sienkiewicz**

She says nothing.

Every morning her mother dresses her,

because the alternative is not to touch her, ever,

and her mother even talks to her,

although she never says a word in reply,

Every day her mother walks her across the room,

and sits her in a chair,

puts on the music she liked best before it happened.

Nothing changes.

And somewhere in the back of her head...

...she can hear herself screaming.

HE JUST SAW A BIRD FLY INTO A WINDOW.

IT DID NOT STOP. IT FLEW INTO A WINDOW AS IF IT WERE FLYING INTO THE SKY.

IT WAS HIGH ABOVE HIM BUT HE STILL HEARD THE THUMP AS IT HIT THE GLASS.

Suicide

THERE WAS A DOG NEARBY THE BIRD FELL INTO THE STREET AND THE MOMEN IT FELL HE KNEW THAT I MUST HAVE HAD A MESSAG FOR HIM ATTACHED TO IT LEG.

Suicide Bird Eaten

HE HAS TO HUNT FOR THE BIRD.

IT WAS AN IMPORTANT MESSAGE, ABOUT THE A.M.A. OR THE CITY OFFICIALS.

HE KNOWS TOO MANY THINGS.

IT KILLED ITSELF TO STOP THE FROM FINDING OUT ABOUT HIM.

My mission is to Chronicle them.

Never leave my room until midnight while I chronicle the Sky-boys and their journey through Hells Infinite six thousand pages to date never make less than ten pages a day each day I fail to achieve ten pages I smack my private places with a ruler to chastise myself the weakness of the flesh the pain and without me the sky-boys will be lost.

If I don't chronicle them the little Boys will be lost in hell forever being tortured by demons with knives and hooks and bandages and rulers.

What am I doing away from my room?

I should be back in my room as Nicholas Sky-Boy leads the rebel forces in an attack on Lord Kiss-&-Shah of Hell and rescues his friends from the party girls.

Without me they could die. Time is passing.

Any idea how many we've got so far?

Sky boys need me.

It blossomed in people who came by and gifted him with mushrooms or acid or peyote or home-brewed absinthe until everything picked up a rainbow tint that has never entirely left: his life is the color of childhood.

He has books by Dick. Recently he has taken to encasing himself in silver foil before he goes to sleep.

The third eye. You spend years doing everything you can to open it and then the damn thing opens and your friends laugh at you when you tell them you can see their souls behind their eyes burning like rainbows.

Then the fourth eye opened and the fifth and the ones on the tips of his fingers and everything rainbows at the edges...

He has to go.

Somewhere in the back of her head he is still on top of her, pressing down on her face so she can't breathe (and she's thinking about all the things she's never been and deciding coldly that it would just be smarter right now to be crazy or to be nothing, life and life only) and after that it all got too hard to hold onto.

"I said any idea how many you got?"

"Four. Perhaps five.

That's all? In a city this size?

"I put the call out, Barnabas. I can do no more. There may be more of them out there, but these are the ones who heard.

"They are coming to us."

"LESS THAN HALF A DOZEN CRAZIES. WE DON'T EVEN KNOW THAT THIS WILL WORK."

They are all we have, Matthew. That, and hope.

Okay, team. Listen up. There's somebody in big trouble, and you are our crack troops. No pun intended.
Through that door is a girl. She's hurt. You have to go in and bring her back. Any questions?
THIS GIRL. WAS THAT WHAT THE SUICIDE BIRD KNEW? WERE YOU THE DOG?
Uh. Can I get back to you on that one? Anyone else?
IS THIS ABOUT THE RAINBOWS?
Could well be. Okay, people. Just remember. Little girl. Hurting. We have to get her out. Okay?
Can we head into the bathroom? Keep toward the wall, and please try to stay together.

WHAT DO YOU THINK?

I confess, they do not fill me with confidence.

Yeah. But could you or I go in there when she's in this kind of shape?

No, friend dog. I do not believe that any of us could enter and return with our minds intact.

Is not talking. Does not know where she is. GET OFF, she wanted to say, GET OFF ME, but his hand was over her face and banging her forehead so hard against the wall and that was when she realized it was easier to slip inside.

She's still inside.

What she wants to know is this.

Why are so many people inside with her?

HE PULLS OUT A SHARPIE AND COMMENCES TO WRITE AS THEY GO. *The suicide bird knew they hurt her. Do not paint over this message.*

AS HE WRITES THE FORMS BENEATH HIS WORDS STOP WRITHING AND HOLD THEIR SHAPE.

HE LEAVES A TRAIL OF MESSAGES BEHIND HIM...

She opens her mouth and fishes come out. Not just one fish. Hundreds, maybe. It's liberating, knowing that they are leaving her, but it also makes her feel lonely.

"You know men have babies?"

"Everybody knows men have babies," they all tell her as they twinkle off across the sky.

"There's a girl," she tells them. "She's hurt."

Stella!

"We know about that," they tell her, sadly. Then they begin to sing. She didn't know that fish songs were so lovely.

There were such wonderful things inside her. Who knew? Who could have known?

"Hey, Mom! Guess what I am! A Carcharadon carcharias!"

114

Know where I am of course. This is the hell I wrote about in volume 24 of the Skyboy saga, the Hell of Kenn'edy, named not after the president, a good Catholic and I'm damned sure that's why they shot him, but for a boy I met once.

Years back I put up a display of art in the basement of the school where I work. I put a notice up on the board ART SHOW TODAY, JANITOR'S BASEMENT, and by afternoon someone had taken it down and I found it in the garbage bin that night and I uncrumpled it before I burned it, but even so.

Still, after school a boy came down to my basement and he said "is this where the art show is?" and I said yes, and the boy walked about so gravely looking at the pictures of the Sky-boys as they made their way across the seventeen Hells and at the end he just said "Thank you."

I said, what's your name?

He said, "Brian Kennedy."

Next day the vice-principal pulled me to one side. "No more art shows," he said. Damn near broke my heart.

I tell them all, "This way," when they falter.

Sky-boys lead us onward. Sky-boys fight for us.

I tell them, there's a girl who's hurt.

They say We know! We know! This way! This way!

THEY GET OUT, FOLLOWING A TRAIL OF MESSAGES THAT HANG IN THE SHIFTING WORLDS:

have no truck with the suicide birds IS ONE SUCH MESSAGE.

THEY ARE WRITTEN ON BLURS AND ON AFTERIMAGES AND ON THE AIR.

BABIES RIDING SILVER LIZARDS SEE THEM SAFELY THROUGH THE DARKNESS.

THE LIZARDS SING THE MOST BEAUTIFUL SONGS ANY OF THEM HAVE EVER HEARD.

HE HAS NO JOY IN HIS HEART. HIS MESSAGES WERE HEARD.

She knows the music the fishes sing. She croons that music, sadly, knowing that once your fishes leave you, they can never come back.

First tonight the ruler, to punish myself for walking out without doing the work

He has peace in his soul. All his imaginings are knowledge. He will preach the silver. He will spread the gospel of the rainbow.

Then the Sky-boys. Ten pages still. Maybe twelve. I have hundreds of pages to write and draw befor I can die, and it hurts more and more every day.

They're coming home.

IT'S OKAY. I HURT TOO. HOLD MY HAND.

And then they are back in the crumbling townhouse in the winter and the two girls are still holding each other tightly, as if they never want to let each other go.

AM I... AM I HERE? I WAS SUCH A LONG WAY INSIDE...

Welcome back.

HELLO, DOGGIE.

You scared us. Don't *do* that.

I HURTED.

"SOMEONE MUST HAVE *TAKEN* HER."

"COULDN'T SHE HAVE JUST WANDERED AWAY, MA'AM?"

"NO! SHE...I'M SORRY. SHE'S BEEN NEARLY CATATONIC FOR OVER A YEAR...YOU DON'T JUST GET UP AND WALK..."

HI, MOM. I'M HOME.

119

Chapter 6
DESTRUCTION
On the Peninsula

Chapter 6
DESTRUCTION
On the Peninsula
art by **Glenn Fabry**

I HAD BEEN HAVING BAD DREAMS.

IN SOME OF THEM THE WORLD WAS COVERED BY RISING WATER, IN SOME BY ICE.

SOMETIMES CITIES WOULD BURN, IN MY DREAMS, WHILE ARMED MOBS CROSSED THE COUNTRYSIDE, TAKING WHAT THEY COULD CARRY.

I HAD DREAMS IN WHICH NEW DISEASES AND OLD PLAGUES CHASED EACH OTHER ACROSS THE LAND, WHOLE TABLEAUS IN WHICH NOTHING MOVED, ONLY FLIES CIRCLING CORPSES THAT NOT EVEN THE CARRION-EATERS WOULD TOUCH.

EVERY NIGHT THE DREAMS GREW WORSE.

SOMETIMES THEY EVEN CREPT INTO MY DAY.

"YOU NEED A CHANGE."

IT REALLY IS THE END OF THE WORLD HERE.

I GUESS I MEAN THAT IN MOST WAYS YOU *CAN* MEAN IT. PEOPLE WHO END UP HERE AREN'T GOING ANY FURTHER.

WE'RE KEEPING THE SITE AND ITS NATURE CONFIDENTIAL. OTHERWISE WE LAY OURSELVES OPEN TO *RIDICULE.*

BUT I GOTTA TELLYA, ONCE THE SITE IS FULLY EXCAVATED AND DOCUMENTED, WE WILL SHAKE ARCHAEOLOGY TO ITS FOUNDATIONS--MAYBE SOME OTHER SCIENCES AS WELL.

COME *ON,* STANLEY...ON AN ISLAND THAT'S SEEN NOTHING BUT GOATS AND A COUPLE OF BUSHES SINCE THE DAWN OF TIME?

SAN RAPHAEL'S A PENINSULA. NOT AN ISLAND.

HERE WE ARE. WHAT DO YOU *THINK* OF IT?

IT'S A HILL. WHAT / IT, A *BURIAL MOUND?*

IN A WAY.

FOR A START, IT WASN'T HERE A YEAR AGO.

COME ON, STANLEY. YOU MUST ADMIT THAT SOUNDS A BIT UNLIKELY.

NO, RACHEL. THAT'S NOT UNLIKELY. *THIS* IS UNLIKELY.

IN THE EVENING WE TAKE THE BOAT ACROSS THE BAY TO THE ONLY TOWN, ALSO CALLED SAN RAPHAEL. THERE'S A RESTAURANT/CAFÉ/BAR THERE.

THE LOCALS EYE US WITH AMUSEMENT, BUT OUR MONEY IS GOOD.

AND THE LOCAL WINE IS GOOD, AND CHEAP, AND IT GOES DOWN LIKE LEMONADE.

WE ARE NOT THE ONLY FOREIGNERS ON THE PENINSULA.

WHO ARE *THEY?* TOURISTS?

I GUESS SO. THEY'VE BEEN HERE FOR SEVERAL MONTHS-- THEY'VE GOT A TENT DOWN AT THE END OF THE PENINSULA. THEY WERE HERE WHEN I GOT HERE.

TOURISTS, GYPSIES, HIPPIES. WHO CARES?

HE'S CUTE.

SHE'S TOO YOUNG FOR HIM.

MAYBE SHE'S HIS DAUGHTER, BILL.

MAYBE.

LIKE I SAID. THE WINE WENT DOWN LIKE LEMONADE.

HELLO.

HELLO.

DO YOU NEED TO GET THAT OUT IN ONE PIECE?

I'VE BEEN WORKING ON IT ALL MORNING.

DO YOU MIND...?

OF COURSE I DO. I'M A PROFESSIONAL, I ALMOST SAY.

AND PLEASE, THE WORST THING FOR SITES LIKE THIS IS AMATEURS TRYING TO EXCAVATE THEM...

AND HE CIRCLES MY HANDS WITH HIS GIANT HANDS, AND THEN LIGHTLY, HE TAPS...

THERE.

HEY.

HAVE YOU HAD ANY EXPERIENCE? WITH RUINS?

I'VE CERTAINLY MADE MY SHARE OF THEM.

NO, REALLY. DO YOU NEED A JOB?

YOU WHAT?

I ASKED HIM TO HELP. WE NEED HELP. BILL'S USELESS.

HMPH.

CAT N° 1375

I DID NOT DREAM THAT NIGHT...THEN AGAIN, I DIDN'T GET A LOT OF SLEEP. SO I TYPED, AND I WORKED. ON MY OWN.

HE WAS ALREADY THERE AT 8 A.M. THAT MORNING, WHEN I GOT DOWN TO THE DIG.

WE WORKED TOGETHER, EXCAVATING A CACHE OF FOSSILIZED MAGAZINES.

THEY CRUMBLED TO POWDER AS WE PULLED THEM OUT, ALTHOUGH THE COVER OF THE TOPMOST MAGAZINE WAS IMPRINTED, REVERSED, ON THE TOP LAYER. ƎMIꞆ WAS THE MAGAZINE. IT WARNED OF !ЯⱯW.

AT THE END OF THE WEEK, WE FOUND THINGS THAT MIGHT HAVE BEEN BULLETS. ALL OF THEM WERE SPENT EXCEPT FOR ONE, WHICH GLOWED BLUE WHEN I TOUCHED IT.

LOOK AT THIS!

A PRICELESS ARTEFACT OF THE FUTURE. AND IT GLOWS!

OW...

WHAT... WHAT **WAS** THAT?

IT WAS A HUNTER-KILLER SLUG. STILL LIVE.

HOW DID YOU **KNOW?**

THEY'RE LIKE KNIVES OR CLUBS. THE PATTERNS ARE DIFFERENT, BUT THE PURPOSE OF THE OBJECT IS OBVIOUS.

THE BIG GUY DIDN'T SHOW UP FOR WORK THE NEXT DAY. HE WASN'T AT THE CAFÉ IN THE EVENING.

WHERE'S YOUR FRIEND?

HE WENT FOR A WALK.

OH.

I DON'T KNOW WHERE HE WENT FOR A WALK. HE HASN'T GONE VERY FAR. HE HAS TO STAY SORT OF NEAR ME FOR A BIT. THEY ASKED HIM TO KEEP AN EYE ON ME. THE REST OF MY FAMILY.

WHY?

BECAUSE... BECAUSE I WAS SICK. I GUESS... THEY DON'T WANT ME TO BE ON MY OWN.

YOU KNOW WHY THE THING, THE HILL, THE PLACE YOU'RE DIGGING IS THERE?

NO.

IT'S BECAUSE OF ME. OR BECAUSE OF HIM, MAYBE. OR BOTH OF US. I GUESS IT'S BOTH OF US, REALLY. BEING HERE. THAT DOES IT.

135

IT'S NOT FROM THE **FUTURE**, YOU SEE.

IT'S **NOT**?

NO...OR MAYBE IT IS.

BUT JUST A BIT OF **ONE** OF THEM. I MEAN, THERE ARE SO **MANY** OF THEM. LIKE WIGGLY WORMS, MILLIONS AND BILLIONS AND SQUILLIONS OF WIGGLY WORMS, ALL WIGGLING IN DIFFERENT WAYS TO GET TO THE SAME PLACE.

AND I KNOW WHAT THAT PLACE IS.

IT'S A NOTHING PLACE. AND MY SISTER WILL TAKE MY BROTHER'S BOOK AND SAY GOODBYE, LIKE THIS, "GOODBYE," AND THEN IT'S ALL DONE. AND THAT'S IT FOR THIS TIME ROUND.

YOU DON'T BELIEVE ME. BUT I DON'T MIND. I DON'T ALWAYS BELIEVE ME EITHER.

I SHOULD BE GETTING BACK. DO YOU HAVE A FLASHLIGHT?

NO.

I HAVE LIGHTNING BUGS, THOUGH. WOULD YOU LIKE THEM?

CUTE. WHEN I WAS A KID I PUT FIREFLIES IN A JAR...

THEY AREN'T IN A JAR. THEY ARE IN THE BUSHES. BUT THEY WILL FOLLOW YOU BACK TO THE DIG, SINGING LITTLE FIREFLY SONGS, LALALA, IF YOU LIKE.

WHAT'S YOUR BROTHER'S **NAME**?

WHAT?

YOUR **BROTHER**. HE'S BEEN WORKING FOR US FOR A WEEK NOW. WE HAVE TO PUT HIM DOWN ON THE PAYROLL RECORDS.

THAT IS A VERY GOOD QUESTION, YOU KNOW. I DON'T KNOW, REALLY. I MEAN, I KNOW WHAT IT USED TO BE. I DON'T KNOW IF HE IS THAT ANYMORE. I MEAN, HE KNOWS IF I'M TALKING TO HIM IT'S HIM I'M TALKING TO...

...MAYBE YOU JUST BETTER OUGHT TO CALL HIM JOE.

IS THAT HIS **NAME**?

OH **NO**. NOT EVEN A LITTLE BIT.

WELL, IT WAS GOOD TALKING TO YOU.

HELLO. I SPOKE TO YOUR SISTER.

I *THOUGHT* YOU MIGHT HAVE DONE.

SHE SAID I SHOULD CALL YOU JOE.

SHE *DID*, DID SHE? WELL, PERHAPS SHE'S FEELING *BETTER*.

WHAT HAPPENED TO HER?

HARD TO *SAY*. SHE WON'T TELL ANYONE. I THINK SHE GOT HER FEELINGS HURT, AND SHE WENT TOO DEEPLY INSIDE HERSELF.

WHEN YOU'RE THAT AGE IT'S TOO EASY TO GET YOUR HEART BROKEN. I REMEMBER.

HMM... DO *YOU* THINK THAT'S WHAT IT WAS?

YOU WANT TO KNOW SOMETHING *WEIRD?* SHE SAID THAT SHE DIDN'T HAVE A FLASHLIGHT. AND THAT THE LIGHTNING BUGS WOULD FOLLOW ME BACK HERE.

AND THEY *DID*.

I'M SURE THEY DID.

GOODNIGHT, JOE. SEE YOU TOMORROW.

GOODNIGHT.

AND HIS HUGE HAND CLOSED AROUND MINE.

AND I WENT BACK TO MY TENT, ALONE.

I WAS WOKEN BY HELICOPTERS.

"THESE PEOPLE WANT TO *WHAT?*"

I *TOLD* YOU, MA'AM. SEND IN THE *BULLDOZERS.*

THERE ARE ISOTOPES IN THE SAMPLES YOU SENT BACK...

...THAT WE'VE ONLY BEEN ABLE TO MAKE IN *LABORATORIES* UNTIL NOW.

THE STATE DEPARTMENT HAS DONE A DEAL WITH ONE OF THE BIG CHEMICAL COMPANIES TO TAKE THE ENTIRE HILL. THEIR PAPERS ARE IN ORDER.

BUT THAT HILL'S *PRICELESS.*

EXACTLY, DOCTOR. IT'S PRICELESS.

BUT WE'RE EXCAVATING THE FUTURE.

MA'AM, HAS IT OCCURRED TO YOU, THAT IF THE CONTENTS OF THAT MOUND FALLS INTO THE WRONG HANDS, THERE MAY NOT *BE* ANY FUTURE?

BECAUSE *THEY'LL* MAKE WEAPONS OUT OF THEM, AND YOU *WON'T?*

REMEMBER THE SECOND WORLD WAR. SOMETIMES THE RIGHT WEAPON IN THE RIGHT HANDS CAN SAVE *MILLIONS* OF LIVES.

YOU KNOW, THERE ARE OBJECTS IN THAT HILL. THINGS FROM THE FUTURE. *DANGEROUS* THINGS.

WE'RE FROM THE GOVERNMENT. WE *KNOW* WHAT WE'RE DOING.

SURE YOU DO.

STANLEY, I DON'T WANT TO BE HERE WHILE THIS IS HAPPENING. I'M GOING BACK TO THE MAINLAND.

THIS IS A CLASSIFIED SITE, MA'AM. I *FORBID* YOU TO LEAVE--

YOU'RE HERE AS A REPRESENTATIVE OF A CHEMICAL COMPANY. *I'M* AN ACADEMIC ON FOREIGN SOIL.

AND A THREE THOUSAND WORD DESCRIPTION OF THIS PLACE AND THE ARTEFACTS WE'VE UN-EARTHED WILL BE SENT TO SLASHDOT.ORG BY A ROBOT UNLESS I GET ONLINE AND CANCEL IT TONIGHT. YOU CAN'T FORBID ME *ANYTHING.*

I'M DISAPPOINTED IN YOU, RACHEL.

SORRY, STANLEY.

HEY!

I SAW THEM ACROSS THE SQUARE, IN THE TOWN ON THE MAINLAND, SO THEY MUST HAVE GOTTEN OUT TOO. I WAS PLEASED.

BUT THEY'D GONE BY THE TIME I GOT TO THE CAFÉ.

SO I SAT DOWN IN THE CAFÉ, AND I ORDERED A GLASS OF RED WINE, AND I STARED ACROSS THE BAY, AND THOUGHT ABOUT THE BULLDOZERS CRASHING INTO THE SIDE OF THE HILL...

I WONDER WHAT IT WAS THAT DID IT. ANOTHER HUNTER-KILLER SLUG? OR SOMETHING ELSE, SOME OTHER WEAPON FROM A WAR WE'VE NOT YET FOUGHT.

WHATEVER IT WAS, IT WAS CLEAN. ONE FLASH OF LIGHT AND THE PENINSULA WAS GONE.

AN EARTHQUAKE, THEY SAID IN ONE OF THE PAPERS. OR AN UNDERSEA VOLCANO. BUT MOST PAPERS DIDN'T SAY ANYTHING.

NOBODY KNOWS. NOBODY CARES.

Bread Cakes

THERE'S A PENINSULA WITH THE FUTURE ON IT THAT ISN'T THERE ANY MORE.

I'VE HEARD NOTHING. NO MEN IN BLACK HAVE TURNED UP TO TAKE ME AWAY.

AND NOW, WHEN I DREAM, IT IS OF THE VOICE OF A MAN ABOUT WHOM THE ONLY THING I KNOW FOR SURE IS THAT HIS NAME ISN'T JOE, AND OF HIS HUGE HANDS CLOSING AROUND MINE.

HIS HANDS, THAT WRAPPED AROUND MINE AS SURELY AND FIRMLY AS THE FUTURE HOLDS TODAY.

END

Chapter 7 **DESTINY**
— Endless Nights

DESTINY

Endless Nights

art by **Frank Quitely**

There is a man with a book,
walking through his garden.

The man
is blind.

The garden is a maze
of paths that divide
and branch and recombine.

There are statues in the garden. Huge statues. If they move, as some claim they do, it is too slowly to be easily perceived.

The book is heavy. You would not be able to lift it.

Now his path takes him into his dwelling, a place of corridors and halls.

The paintings in Destiny's hall show his brothers and sisters as they might wish to be seen (although the wish and the thing are so close in the realm of the Endless that you cannot get a thin-bladed knife between them).

You will spend time in the realm of each of his siblings — you will dream, despair, desire, destroy, delight and otherwise, and, eventually, die — but you were his from the very first page, and only he will read how your story comes out, a long time from now.

He is chained to the book, or it is chained to him. It is a book of many pages. It cannot be stolen; he cannot give it away.

It contains your life. Every detail of your life. Everything that has happened to you. Everything that will happen one day. The things you've forgotten.

The things you don't believe.

It contains everything that has happened, or will happen, to anyone you've ever met.

Anyone you've ever heard of.

Anyone you've never heard of.

The histories and the dreams and triumphs of the dead are there.

The meaning of the patterns of the spots of each leopard is written there, along with the truth of the shapes of clouds, and the strange, funny song-lives of the bacteria-folk and the secrets the wind whispers when there is no one there to listen.

Everything is in there, from the beginning of time to the end.

He did not create the path you walk.

But the movements of atoms and galaxies are in his book, and he sees little difference between them.

It is all in his book. One day he will lay it down, when the book is done, and what comes after that is still unwritten.

A page turns.

Destiny
continues
to walk...

He is holding a book.
Inside the book is
the Universe.

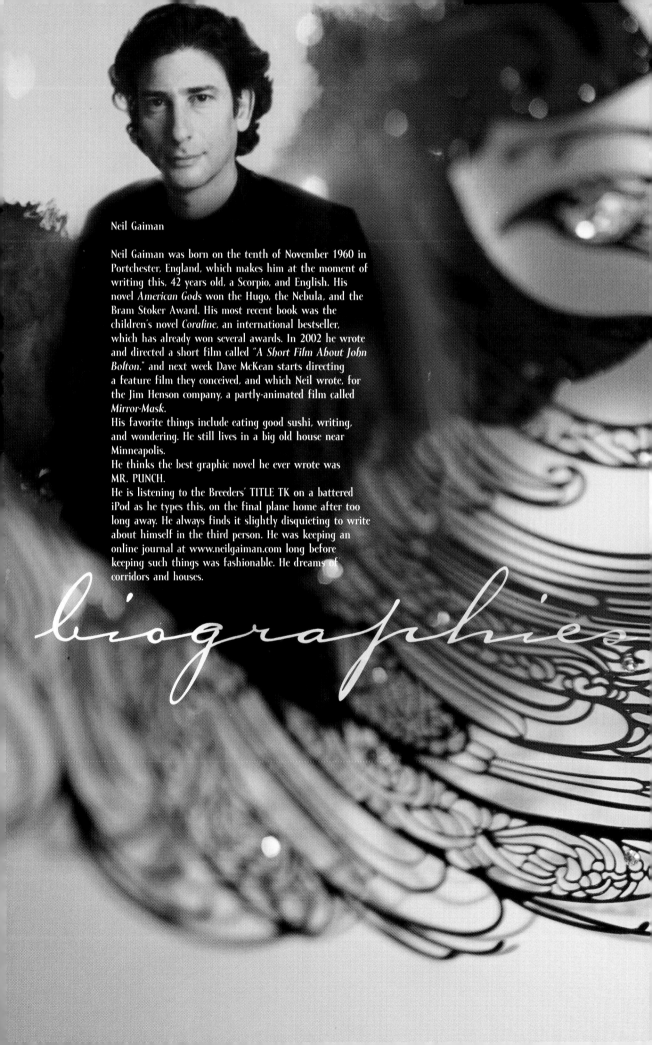

Neil Gaiman

Neil Gaiman was born on the tenth of November 1960 in
Portchester, England, which makes him at the moment of
writing this, 42 years old, a Scorpio, and English. His
novel *American Gods* won the Hugo, the Nebula, and the
Bram Stoker Award. His most recent book was the
children's novel *Coraline*, an international bestseller,
which has already won several awards. In 2002 he wrote
and directed a short film called "*A Short Film About John
Bolton*," and next week Dave McKean starts directing
a feature film they conceived, and which Neil wrote, for
the Jim Henson company, a partly-animated film called
Mirror-Mask.
His favorite things include eating good sushi, writing,
and wondering. He still lives in a big old house near
Minneapolis.
He thinks the best graphic novel he ever wrote was
MR. PUNCH.
He is listening to the Breeders' TITLE TK on a battered
iPod as he types this, on the final plane home after too
long away. He always finds it slightly disquieting to write
about himself in the third person. He was keeping an
online journal at www.neilgaiman.com long before
keeping such things was fashionable. He dreams of
corridors and houses.

biographies

Miguelanxo Prado

I was born in 1958 in A Coruna, a Galician city in Spain by the seacoast of the Atlantic Ocean, in the Europeans land's end.

I had begun studying architecture but finally decided to leave it and engage in what I have always been passionate about, to paint and to write. I also create music, but 24 hours in a day was not enough time for everything, and I have left music. I started working in comics in the early eighties and I'm still painting.

I illustrate books, collaborate in the press, do artistic direction for TV, character creation for the *Men in Black* cartoon series, and I engage myself in any project that looks appealing and is related to the world of image and storytelling.

For my work I use traditional means: pencils, pens, paintbrushes, paintings of every kind; but I have also been persuaded to use new technologies. I live in the country; I like to travel, to read, and to listen to music, to watch movies and to share good wine and good conversation with my friends.

And I wouldn't be able to live far from the sea for a long time.

Soon he became a master class artist and found critical acclaim even from the hard-to-please, cultured Italian readers still stunned by the graphic and narrative revolution of *Metal Hurlant* the French magazine which featured Manara's contemporaries such as Moebius, Druillet, and Caza. Manara made his debut drawing the epic Buddhist adventures of *Lo Scimmiotto*, written by Silverio Pisu. Struck by the style of Moebius, Manara experimented with his style and improved upon it for his next work, *Alessio Borghese Rivoluzionario*. While the erotic charge and sexual irony of Manara's work have made him one of the world's premier illustrators, the overlooked qualities of his simple and attractive scenarios have made him an honest, artistic reporter of his times, through escapist literature and the erotic tale. His books have gained international success and include such titles as *Clik*, the playbills for Fellini's *L'intervista*, and many political and satirical shorts and comic strips.

Milo Manara

Manara, one of the best-known Italian illustrators, was the ideal heir of Hugo Pratt who was his friend, master, and in some ways, agent. Manara started illustrating in the seventies on pulp magazines for adult readers.

Barron Storey

Who is Barron Storey? He's a good fellow, from a good family, who's done a lot of good work and taught a lot of good students including painters Kent Williams, George Pratt, John Van Fleet, and Seth among others. Along the way Barron discovered that something was not quite right about himself. He's been working that out for many years in the only way he knows how: through making art.

Winner of the NY Society of Illustrators Gold Medal in 1976, Barron has taught at many universities including the School of Visual Arts in New York City and Art Center College of Design. He's worked as a freelance illustrator for diverse clients from the United States Information Agency and NASA to *Heavy Metal* and Putnam Publishing. As an exhibiting artist, Barron has held many one-man shows in New York City and Washington, DC. Also active in theatre and music, he resides in San Francisco.

Glenn Fabry

When I was a little kid my dearest wish was to be a comic book artist, ideally for DC or *Marvel*. Well, let's face it, I wasn't good enough at seven, it wasn't going to happen. But the years passed, hair grew in unexpected places (once on the back of the toaster at my Granny's) and by 1984 I was drawing *Slaine* (by the great Pat Mills) for *2000 A.D.* in Britain. By 1992, I was painting covers for HELLBLAZER and later, PREACHER (by the estimable Garth Ennis) for DC/VERTIGO. My ambition had finally been realized: To sit in a room drawing for 20 years!
Well, it makes me happy.

Todd Klein

Todd Klein has been lettering comics since 1977. A highlight of his career is his work with Neil Gaiman on nearly all the original issues of THE SANDMAN, as well as BLACK ORCHID, DEATH and THE BOOKS OF MAGIC. Currently he is teamed with Alan Moore on all the AMERICA'S BEST COMICS titles, Frank Miller on DK2, Linda Medley on *Castle Waiting* and Bill Willingham on FABLES, among others. Todd has won numerous Eisner and Harvey Awards for his work.

P. Craig Russell

P. Craig Russell is a 31-year veteran of the comics biz. His work ranges from superhero (BATMAN, *Dr. Strange*) to fantasy (THE SANDMAN, *Elric*) to adaptations of classic literature and opera (*The Magic Flute, The Ring of the Nibelung*). He is currently (11 years and counting) adapting *The Complete Fairy Tales of Oscar Wilde*. ENDLESS NIGHTS: Death in Venice is his fourth collaboration with Neil Gaiman.

Bill Sienkiewicz

Bill Sienkiewicz has had a major impact on the field of comic books with his innovative use of collage, illustration techniques and story-telling. He has won nearly every major award in the U.S. and abroad, and has exhibited his art worldwide. Among his best known works are the series *Elektra: Assassin* for which he received the prestigious Yellow Kid Award, and the critically acclaimed *Stray Toasters* which he wrote and illustrated. He was nominated for two Emmy awards for his work on the animated series *Where in the World is Carmen San Diego?* and he also worked on the film *Unforgiven*. Currently Bill is working on a web project for the creators of *The Matrix* and a BATMAN miniseries.

Frank Quitely

Frank Quitely was born in Glasgow in 1968. During the period 1988-2003 he's drawn *The Greens* (self-published), *Blackheart*, *Missionary Man*, *Shimura*, *Inaba*, Ten *Paradox Press* shorts, Six VERTIGO shorts, FLEX MENTALLO, 20/20 VISIONS, BATMAN: THE SCOTTISH CONNECTION, THE KINGDOM: OFFSPRING, JLA: EARTH 2 hardcover, THE INVISIBLES, TRANSMETROPOLITAN, THE AUTHORITY, *Captain America*, *New X-Men* and now THE SANDMAN. He lives in Glasgow with his wife and two sons. He used to design his own hats and clothing. Currently, his favourite hobby is cooking. He's known to make a mean pesto.

Dave McKean

McKean has illustrated several award-winning comics including the best-selling ARKHAM ASYLUM (written by Grant Morrison), MR. PUNCH, *Signal To Noise* and *Violent Cases* (all written by Neil Gaiman), *Slow Chocolate Autopsy* (written by Iain Sinclair) and his own *Cages*. His collected short stories *Pictures that Tick* recently won the Victoria & Albert Museum Book of the Year Award, and his last short film *N[eon]* won overall first prize at the Claremont Ferrand Film Festival.

McKean has illustrated, photographed and designed over 150 CD covers and hundreds of comic and book covers including the entire SANDMAN series. He has worked on print and film projects with John Cale, Stephen King, The Rolling Stones, Lars Von Trier and SF Said, and created ad campaigns for Kodak, Nike, BMW Mini, Smirnoff among others.

He runs the jazz label *Feral* with top sax player Iain Ballamy, and has contributed production design to the second and third *Harry Potter* films. McKean lives in the Kent countryside in the UK.

The Sandman Library

Ten definitive graphic novels that reveal the story of Morpheus and the Endless, his uniquely dysfunctional family.

Preludes & Nocturnes

Dream of the Endless, also known as the Sandman, had been trapped for 70 years. After his imprisonment and eventual escape, the Sandman must reclaim his realm, The Dreaming, as well as his articles of power: his helmet, his pouch and his amulet.

The Doll's House

Rose Walker finds more than she bargained for including long lost relatives, a serial killers' convention and, ultimately, her true identity when The Sandman attempts to unravel her mystery.

Dream Country

Four chilling and unique tales: *Calliope, Dream of a Thousand Cats, Façade,* and *A Midsummer Night's Dream,* The World Fantasy Award-winning story of the first performance of William Shakespeare's play with art by Charles Vess. Also contains Gaiman's original comic book script for *Calliope.*

Season of Mists

Ten thousand years ago, the Sandman condemned his one true love to the pits of Hell. When his sister Death convinces him that Nada was unjustly imprisoned, Dream journeys to Hell to rescue his lost lover ... just as Lucifer Morningstar decides to abdicate his throne... leaving the Key to Hell in the hands of the Sandman.

A Game of You

Barbie, from The Doll's House, used to dream of being a princess in a lush, private kingdom with strange animals as her subjects. But Barbie has stopped dreaming. Now her imaginary world and her real world entwine in a riveting story about gender and identity.

Fables & Reflections

From the mists of the past to the nightmares of the present, Dream touches the lives of Haroun Al Raschid, King of Ancient Baghdad, Lady Johanna Constantine, spy and adventuress, and Joshua Norton, self-styled emperor of the United States, among others in nine remarkable self-contained stories.

Brief Lives

Delirium, youngest of the Endless, prevails upon her brother Dream to help find their missing brother, Destruction. Their odyssey through the waking world also leads the Sandman to resolve his painful relationship with his son, Orpheus.

Worlds' End

Caught in the vortex of a reality storm, wayfarers from throughout time, myth and the imagination converge on a mysterious inn. In the tradition of Chaucer's Canterbury Tales, the travelers wait out the tempest that rages around them by sharing stories.

The Kindly Ones

Frightened people called them The Kindly Ones. Unstoppable in their mission of vengeance, they would not rest until the crime they sought to punish had been avenged; had been washed clean, with blood. Now Dream of the Endless, his acquaintances and his family find themselves caught up in a dark conspiracy. And someone is going to die.

The Wake

Ancient gods, old friends and enemies gather to pay tribute, and to remember, in the strangest wake ever held. And, at the end of his life, William Shakespeare fulfills his side of a very strange bargain.

Related Titles:

The Sandman: The Dream Hunters

Set in Japan, this adult fairytale, told in single illustration and prose, is beautifully painted by legendary artist Yoshitaka Amano.

Death: The High Cost of Living

One day every century, Death takes on mortal form to learn more about the lives she must take.

Death: The Time of Your Life

When a young mother makes a deal with Death to save her young son, her girlfriend pays the price in a story about fame, relationships and rock and roll.

Books about THE SANDMAN

The Sandman Companion – by Hy Bender

Dust Covers – The Collected SANDMAN Covers 1989 – 1997

The Quotable Sandman

The Sandman – King of Dreams

Other great collections from Vertigo:
All Vertigo titles are Suggested for Mature Readers

NEIL GAIMAN AND CHARLES VESS' STARDUST
Neil Gaiman/Charles Vess

NEIL GAIMAN'S MIDNIGHT DAYS
Neil Gaiman/various

BLACK ORCHID
Neil Gaiman/Dave McKean

MR. PUNCH
Neil Gaiman/Dave McKean

THE BOOKS OF MAGIC
Neil Gaiman/various

THE BOOKS OF MAGIC: BINDINGS
John Ney Rieber/Gary Amaro/Peter Gross

THE BOOKS OF MAGIC: SUMMONINGS
John Ney Rieber/various

THE BOOKS OF MAGIC: RECKONINGS
John Ney Rieber/various

THE BOOKS OF MAGIC: TRANSFORMATIONS
John Ney Rieber/Peter Gross

THE BOOKS OF MAGIC: GIRL IN THE BOX
John Ney Rieber/Peter Gross/Peter Snejbjerg

THE BOOKS OF MAGIC: THE BURNING GIRL
John Ney Rieber/Peter Gross/Peter Snejbjerg

THE BOOKS OF MAGIC: DEATH AFTER DEATH
John Ney Rieber/various

THE BOOKS OF FAERIE
Bronwyn Carlton/John Ney Rieber/Peter Gross

THE BOOKS OF FAERIE: AUBERON'S TALE
Bronwyn Carlton/John Ney Rieber/various

THE NAMES OF MAGIC
Dylan Horrocks/Richard Case

DESTINY: A CHRONICLE OF DEATHS FORETOLD
Alisa Kwitney/various

THE LITTLE ENDLESS STORYBOOK
Jill Thompson

DEATH: AT DEATH'S DOOR
Jill Thompson

FABLES: LEGENDS IN EXILE
Bill Willingham/Lan Medina/
Steve Leialoha/Craig Hamilton

FABLES: ANIMAL FARM
Bill Willingham/Mark Buckingham/
Steve Leialoha

HEAVY LIQUID
Paul Pope

HELLBLAZER: ORIGINAL SINS
Jamie Delano/various

HELLBLAZER: DANGEROUS HABITS
Garth Ennis/various

HELLBLAZER: FEAR AND LOATHING
Garth Ennis/Steve Dillon

HELLBLAZER: TAINTED LOVE
Garth Ennis/Steve Dillon

HELLBLAZER: DAMNATION'S FLAME
Garth Ennis/Steve Dillon/
William Simpson/Peter Snejbjerg

HELLBLAZER: HAUNTED
Warren Ellis/John Higgins

HELLBLAZER: HARD TIME
Brian Azzarello/Richard Corben

HELLBLAZER: GOOD INTENTIONS
Brian Azzarello/Marcelo Frusin

JONNY DOUBLE
Brian Azzarello/Eduardo Risso

LUCIFER: DEVIL IN THE GATEWAY
Mike Carey/Peter Gross/Chris Weston

LUCIFER: CHILDREN AND MONSTERS
Mike Carey/Peter Gross/Dean Ormston

LUCIFER: A DALLIANCE WITH
THE DAMNED
Mike Carey/Peter Gross/Dean Ormston

LUCIFER: THE DIVINE COMEDY
Mike Carey/Peter Gross/Dean Ormston

100 BULLETS: FIRST SHOT, LAST CALL
Brian Azzarello/Eduardo Risso

100 BULLETS: SPLIT SECOND CHANCE
Brian Azzarello/Eduardo Risso

100 BULLETS: HANG UP ON THE HANG LOW
Brian Azzarello/Eduardo Risso

100 BULLETS: A FOREGONE TOMORROW
Brian Azzarello/Eduardo Risso

100 BULLETS: THE COUNTERFIFTH DETECTIVE
Brian Azzarello/Eduardo Risso

PREACHER: GONE TO TEXAS
Garth Ennis/Steve Dillon

PREACHER: UNTIL THE END OF THE WORLD
Garth Ennis/Steve Dillon

PREACHER: PROUD AMERICANS
Garth Ennis/Steve Dillon

PREACHER: ANCIENT HISTORY
Garth Ennis/Steve Dillon/various

PREACHER: DIXIE FRIED
Garth Ennis/Steve Dillon

PREACHER: WAR IN THE SUN
Garth Ennis/Steve Dillon/Peter Snejbjerg

PREACHER: SALVATION
Garth Ennis/Steve Dillon

PREACHER: ALL HELL'S A-COMING
Garth Ennis/Steve Dillon/John McCrea

PREACHER: ALAMO
Garth Ennis/Steve Dillon

PREACHER: DEAD OR ALIVE
(THE COLLECTED COVERS)
Glenn Fabry

SWAMP THING: DARK GENESIS
Len Wein/Berni Wrightson

SAGA OF THE SWAMP THING
Alan Moore/Stephen Bissette/John Totleben

SWAMP THING: LOVE & DEATH
Alan Moore/Stephen Bissette/
John Totleben/Shawn McManus

SWAMP THING: THE CURSE
Alan Moore/Stephen Bissette/John Totleben

SWAMP THING: A MURDER OF CROWS
Alan Moore/various

SWAMP THING: EARTH TO EARTH
Alan Moore/John Totleben/
Rick Veitch/Alfredo Alcala

SWAMP THING: REUNION
Alan Moore/Rick Veitch/
Stephen Bissette/Alfredo Alcala/
John Totleben/Tom Yeates

TRANSMETROPOLITAN: BACK ON THE STREET
Warren Ellis/Darick Robertson/various

TRANSMETROPOLITAN: LUST FOR LIFE
Warren Ellis/Darick Robertson/various

TRANSMETROPOLITAN: YEAR OF THE BASTARD
Warren Ellis/Darick Robertson/
Rodney Ramos

Y: THE LAST MAN — UNMANNED
Brian K. Vaughan/Pia Guerra/José Marzán, Jr.

To find more collected editions and monthly comic books from DC Comics,
call 1-888-COMIC BOOK for the nearest comics shop or go to your local book store.

Visit us at www.vertigocomics.com